Wicked
TRAVELER

Howard Tomb

WORKMAN PUBLISHING · NEW YORK

Library of Congress Cataloging-in-Publication Data
is available.
ISBN 978-0-7611-3592-0

Workman books are available at special discounts
when purchased in bulk for premiums and sales pro-
motions as well as for fund-raising or educational use.
Special editions or book excerpts can also be created
to specification. For details, contact the Special Sales
Director at the address below or send an e-mail to
specialmarkets@workman.com.

Illustrations by Jared Lee
Cover and book design by Paul Gamarello

Workman Publishing Company, Inc.
225 Varick Street
New York, NY 10014-4381
www.workman.com

Printed in the United States of America

First Printing February 2005

10 9 8 7 6 5 4 3 2

CONTENTS

WICKED JAPANESE

WICKED SPANISH

ACKNOWLEDGMENTS

Many thanks to Jorge Aizenman, John Boswell, Elizabeth Brown, Patty Brown, Michael Cader, Alice, Jack and Therese Davison, Ulrike Dorda, Sophie Gillet, Sally Kovalchick, Gabriel Landau, Ilaria Lemme, Renée Lowther, Kuni Mikami, Carbery O'Brien, Francesco Pansardi, Christine Ruggeri, Ben Stoner, Kao Temma, and Marcela Villanueva.

WELCOME TO A FOREIGN PLACE

Every country is different, but all foreign places
have one thing in common: they're foreign.
Strange sights, sounds, and smells can be
stimulating, but after a few hours they're liable to
make us feel unsettled or even weepy, particularly if
we are unable to obtain a proper cocktail. We don't
want to have to rifle through our bags looking for
the tiny phrasebook that pertains to whatever nation
we happen to have crossed into, cursing under our
breath while the foreigners around us mutate from
bored bureaucrats into belligerent aliens.

That's one reason I've collected five most popular phrasebooks into one heftier volume: it makes it
easier to find. And much more useful when you do.
The countries we cover are so small that you can
end up there almost by accident: getting on the
wrong ski lift, falling asleep on a train, or stowing
away in a hastily chosen container ship.

And while natives anywhere may fail to understand a traveler mangling their language, they all
grasp the potential power of a half-pound (186-gram)
volume in the traveler's fist. This book makes a far
better bludgeon than its slim 64-page sisters. It has

the greatest throw weight of any phrasebook in its price range. And since it's available in nearly every decent bookstore in the United States and Great Britain, it is easily replaced should it become lost, soiled, or seized as evidence in an assault case.

You have my best wishes. *Vaya con huevos.*

Howard Tomb

Wicked

FRENCH

J'essaie de restreindre ma consommation de foie de veau.

I'm trying to cut down on liver from anemic calves.

Shess-ay duh ress-tran-druh mah con-som-ah-SYON duh FWAH duh voh.

CONTENTS

BUREAUCRACY AND CULTURE

WINE AND FOOD

CAFÉS AND NIGHTLIFE

THE MODEL GUEST

WELCOME TO FRANCE

The French believe that they founded Western civilization. In fact, many of them question whether cultural refinement has ever spread beyond the borders of their *beau pays*.

They may have a point. French Cro-Magnons were making superb cave paintings as early as 40,000 B.C. Would anyone be surprised if anthropologists discovered that these artists were also enjoying stinky cheese, foie gras, and Pernod during their gallery openings?

But dwelling too long on French cultural history has risks: it can lead to a sense of inferiority, which in turn can cause a visitor to show weakness. That, my friend, would be un-American.

And it would be wrong.

You are entitled to hospitality and yes, courtesy, from your hosts—even if they *are* French. If you ever begin to doubt your own worth, repeat these words:

- French rock
- French sandwiches
- French army

These phrases have no meaning, of course. And that's the point. A nation that hasn't figured out how to rock the house, make a decent roast beef sandwich, or point a gun in the right direction has no business looking down its lengthy nose at anybody.

Armed with a sense of equality, if not fraternity, you can use the phrases in this book to free yourself of old fears and become a more complete traveler, capable of subtle understanding, effective discourse, and, when necessary, verbal assault.

Bonne chance.

MAKING FRENCH NOISES WITH YOUR MOUTH AND NOSE

A traveler in France may wish to obtain such things as a hotel room, a bottle of beer, or a ticket home. Without the proper accent, such luxuries may not be forthcoming. Frenchmen will feel free to torment you. They may never reveal that they speak English perfectly.

Many of the sounds made by French people are never made by English-speaking mouths. These peculiar noises are therefore difficult to describe

THE UNTRANSLATABLES

The following phrases have no meaning in France. Do not attempt to translate them.

French fries	French Canadian
French bread	French dressing
French pastry	French toast
French cuffs	French leave
French kissing	French doors
French dry cleaning	French windows
French heels	French horn
French restaurant	French poodle
	French letter

and to imitate. Nevertheless, you must attempt to approximate a French accent if you hope to avoid being seen as a creature totally unworthy of respect, *un boucher de la langue sacrée* (a butcher of the holy tongue).

THE *U* IN *STUPIDE*

The *u* in *stupide* is a tough one, but learning it is crucial. Without it, you will be unable to say such things as:

These stinking truffles are overrated.	Ces truffes puantes sont surfaites.	*Say trüf püj–ONT sohn SÿR-fet.*
Stop at my petticoat, Luc, you beastly peasant!!	Ne te rue pas sur mon jupon, Luc, espèce de rustaud brutal!	*Nuh tuh rüj pah sür mohn jüj-POHN, Lüjk, esspess duh RÿS-toh brüj-TAHL!*
This nectarine is very hard.	Ce brugnon est très dur.	*Suh brüjn-YON ay tray düjr.*

Making the sound requires holding the lips out in an O shape, imitating the look of interest sometimes seen on the faces of chimpanzees, while making the sound "eee." It does *not* sound like "ooo." The sound, to our ears, suggests sharp disgust.

The *u* in *stupide* will be designated in the phonetic instructions as *ÿ*.

THE *R* IN *RUDE*

he flat *r* Americans use is painful to Continental
ears. Some French *r*'s are silent, as in the verb
aimer, to love, which is pronounced "AY-may." *R*'s
that are pronounced are blended with the gagging
g sound perfected by Inspector Clouseau.

You may be able to make yourself understood
without a proper *R*, but the thicker your American
accent, the thicker your listeners will assume you
to be.

Practice with the following phrases:

I prefer drinking battery acid to reading Rimbaud.	Je préfère boire l'acide d'une batterie de voiture que lire du Rimbaud.	*Shuh pray-FARE bwarr LAH-seed dÿn bat-ree duh vwah-TŸR kuh leer dÿ ram-BOH.*
The repulsive Citroën burps and bellows like a rhinoceros.	La Citroën rébarbative rote et rugit comme un rhinocéros.	*Lah SEE-troh-en ray-BAR-bah-TEEV rote ay rÿ-JEE cum uhn REE-noh-sair-OSS.*
Okay, Pierre, but be careful not to spoil my hairdo.	D'accord, Pierre, mais garde-toi d'ébouriffer ma coiffure.	*DAK-or, Pyair, may GAR-duh-twah DAY-boor-ee-FAY mah kwah-FŸR.*

THE *N* IN *RIEN*

The French sound for *n* invariably issues from the sinuses. It can be pronounced perfectly well with the mouth closed.

PRONUNCIATION DISCLAIMER

Subtleties of pronunciation must be learned by listening. No book, no matter how cunning or imaginative it may be, can quite describe the sounds made by French people.

The author and publisher take no responsibility for errors of pronunication that result in one or more of the following: any *faux pas* or *gaffe*; the offense of any host or other native; the regrettable consumption of any food or food-like substance; arrival at any (wrong) place at any (wrong) time; or any and all of the tragedies, calamities, inconveniences, and embarrassments traditionally experienced by tone-deaf tourists the world over.

FRIENDLY CUSTOMS AGENTS AND THEIR MACHINE GUNS

ecause of the behavior of certain ruffians and scoundrels, security is tighter than ever at French ports of entry. In evidence at airports are boys who wear bullet-proof vests, tote real machine guns, and whisper commands to their large dogs. The agents and soldiers ignore almost everyone, but woe to the one who attracts their attention.

I'm here for pleasure/business.	Je suis ici pour le plaisir/les affaires.	*Shuh sweez ee-see poor luh play-ZEER/laze ah-FAIR*
I have nothing to declare.	Je n'ai rien à déclarer.	*Shuh nay RYEN ah DAY-clah-RAY.*
Must you open the bags?	Devez-vous ouvrir les bagages?	*DUH-vay-voo oo-vreer lay bah-GAHJ?*
Nice doggie!	Oh le beau toutou!	*Oh luh boh too-TOO!*
Of course, you're welcome to tear my suitcase apart.	Bien sûr, soyez le bienvenu pour réduire ma valise en miettes.	*Byen SŸR, swah-yay luh byen-ven-ÿ poor ray-dweer mah vah-LEEZ on MYET.*

Lucky they're only these tacky Louis Vuitton bags!	Heureusement ce ne sont que des valises moches de Louis Vuitton!	*UR-uz-mon suh nuh sohn kuh day vah-leez mosh duh Loo-ee Vwee-TON!*
No, I didn't pack any Roquefort.	Non, je n'ai pas de Roquefort.	*Nohn, shuh nay PAH duh Roh-keh-FOR.*
I think you smell my socks.	Je pense que ce sont mes chaussettes que vous reniflez.	*Shuh PONCE kuh suh sohn may shoh-SET kuh voo ron-ee-flay.*

PRAYER OF THE FREQUENT FLIER

O Saint Mercury, Mighty Messenger, Lord of Speed, deliver us to the airport on time. Our tickets are no good after this evening. I swear, Your Heavenly Rapidity, I had no idea traffic would be so bad.

Saint-Mercure, Messager Puissant, Seigneur Incontesté de la Vélocité, déposez-nous à temps à notre aéroport. Nos billets ne sont plus valides après ce soir. Je vous jure, o Saint Patron de la Rapidité, que je n'avais aucune idée des embouteillages avec lesquels nous serions confrontés.

TAXI DRIVER

Your life is in his hands. Your heart is in your throat. Isn't Paris exciting? Don't you wish you'd worn diapers?

Most Parisian taxi drivers are not homicidal; they are simply bored. Their own need for adrenaline usually outweighs their concern for their customers' health and happiness.

Whenever you encounter a taxi driver alone, feel free to remind him that he is your servant.

Turn right/left.	Tournez à droite/gauche.	*TOUR-nay ah dwot/goash.*
Where did you learn to drive? Italy?	Où avez-vous appris à conduire? En Italie?	*OO ah-vay voo ah-pree ah con-DWEER? On ee-tal-EE?*
Slow down or die.	Moins vite, ou crève.	*Mwann VEET, oo krev.*

You missed the turn, imbecile!	Vous avez manqué la rue, imbécile!	*Vooz ah-vay mahn-kay lah RŸ, ahm-bay-SEEL!*
Stop here.	Arrêtez-vous ici.	*Ah-ret-ay voo ee-SEE.*
I'll pay only what's on the meter, you idiot.	Je ne payerai que le prix indiqué sur le compteur, espèce d'idiot.	*Shuh nuh pay-er-ay kuh luh pree an-dee-KAY sÿr luh com-TURR, ess-pess dee-DYOH.*
Do you take me for a fool?	Vous me prenez pour un clown?	*Voo muh pruh-nay poor uhn CLOON?*
Don't you know who I am, you numbskull?	Savez-vous qui je suis, cervelle d'oiseau?	*Sav-ay VOO kee shuh SWEE, sair-VEL dwah-ZOH?*
Oh yeah? Your wife says the same thing about you!	Ah oui? Votre femme dit la même chose de vous!	*Ah WEE? Voh-truh FAHM dee lah mem shows duh VOO!*

TAXI DRIVER AVEC CUJO

Parisian drivers are horrifying enough armed only with a car, but some cabs are also equipped with vicious *chiens*. Do not be taken in by small size and an adorable haircut; when such a beast is present, the driver must be treated gingerly. A few French dogs understand English, but they can all smell aggression and fear. Verbal attacks should be subtle or ambiguous.

Drop us off anywhere you like.	Déposez-nous où vous voulez.	*DAY-poh-zay NOO ooh voo VOO-lay.*
Take any route you wish.	Prenez la route que vous préférez.	*PREN-ay lah ROOT kuh voo PRAY-fair-AY.*
I was sure you would kill those pedestrians.	Je savais bien que vous alliez écraser ces piétons.	*Shuh sav-ay BYEN kuh vooz al-yay AY-crah-zay say pyay-TOHN.*
You are a superb driver.	Vous êtes un as du volant.	*Voo-zet uhn NAHSS dÿ voh-lon.*
Have you ever considered a career in auto racing?	Vous n'avez jamais pensé à une carrière de coureur automobile?	*Voo nah-vay SHAM-ay ponce-ay ah ÿn cah-ree-YAIR duh coo-RUR oh-toh-moh-BEEL?*

What a beautiful poodle you have.	Quel beau caniche vous avez là.	*Kell boh can-EESH vooz ah-vay lah.*
I adore fat, cross-eyed dogs.	Je raffole des gros chiens qui louchent.	*Shuh rah-FOHL day grow shee-YEN kee LOOSH.*
Two hundred euros?	Deux cent euros?	*Duh sont you-rohs?*
That sounds reasonable.	Cela semble raisonnable.	*Suh-lah-SOM-bluh RAY-zoh-nah-bluh.*
Of course, it means our vacation ends today.	Bien sûr, cela veut dire que nos vacances se terminent aujourd'hui.	*Byen SŸR, suh-lah vuh deer kuh noh vah-CONCE suh tare-MEEN oh-shore-DWEE.*
It was an honor to ride in your excellent taxi.	Ce fut un honneur de rouler dans votre excellent taxi.	*Suh fÿt uh non-UR duh roo-lay dahn voh-truh EX-ell-ahn tack-SEE.*

KILOMETERS PER HOUR: GET A GRIP

as is so expensive in France that almost everyone has to drive wimpy little cars. This makes motorists feel impotent. They compensate by driving at what are literally breakneck speeds: The preferred highway cruising speed is 215 kilometers per hour (kph), or 133 mph.

Travelers who plan to get behind the wheel should first familiarize themselves with kph and how speed limits apply to various situations.

FRENCH ROAD SIGN	ENGLISH	KPH	MPH
Stop	Stop	60	35
École	School Zone	80	50
Chantier	Men Working	150	95
Virages Dangereux	Hairpin Turns	175	110
Cochon: Attention	Truffle Pig Crossing	200	125
Mouton: Attention	Sheep Crossing	225	140
Prière d'Attacher la Ceinture de Sécurité	Fasten Seat Belt	250	155
Porsche Devant	Porsche Ahead	275	170

RONDPOINT TECHNIQUE AND RECOMMENDED ARMAMENTS

Because the French dislike large intersections, they have developed an alternative: *rondpoints* (roundabouts). This is the Continental form of stock car racing.

Once inside the circle you will find yourself hemmed in by hundreds of tiny, careening cars. Packing a picnic may be a good idea for long afternoons in the *rondpoint*. Remember: food may be projeté (tossed about) inside your vehicle. Avoid fondue dishes.

Sturdy helmets and flameproof suits are helpful. Large-bore pistols, automatic assault rifles, and flame throwers may come in handy when you're ready to clear a path to an exit.

EPITHETS ON WHEELS

Shouting at French drivers in English is profoundly unsatisfying. To elicit expressions of shock and embarrassment from driving opponents, you must communicate with them in their own language.

Hey! Get a license, grandpa!	Hé! Va apprendre à conduire, pépé!	*AY! Vah ah-PRAWN-druh ah con-DWEER, pay-pay!*
Move that worthless heap off the road!	Ôte ce tas de férraille de la circulation!	*Ote suh tah duh fair-EYE duh lah SEER-kÿ-lass yon!*
Which are you? Blind? Or blind drunk?	Quoi? T'es aveugle? Ou complètement bourré?	*Kwah? Tay ah-VUH-gluh? Oo com-plett-mahn boo-RAY?*
Open your eyes, imbecile!	Ouvre les yeux, imbécile!	*OO-vruh lay-ZYUH, am-bay-SEEL!*
Get off my tail, garlic head!	Cesse de me filer le train, tronche d'aïl!	*Sess duh muh fee-lay luh TRAN, tronsh dah-YEE!*
Your mother is Belgian!	Ta mère est belge!	*Tah mare ay BELJH!*

ROAD SIGNS

All motorists must learn to decipher basic road signs. But there are many obscure international symbols that alert the astute driver to cultural hazards and opportunities.

RUDE
SHOPKEEPERS
NEXT 15 KM

SMELLY
FISHERMEN
SMOKING
GAULOISES

NO BERETS

WARNING:
BAD MIME
AHEAD

YET ANOTHER
MATISSE
MUSEUM 1 KM

FINE POINTS OF THE PARIS MÉTRO

On the Paris Métro, certain seats are reserved for war veterans, pregnant women, and so on. These seats are marked for *les anciens combattants.*

When there are too many mothers-to-be and veterans for the number of special seats, a complex system goes into effect. Riders with the fewest remaining limbs get priority. If two veterans have the same number of limbs, World War II veterans are seated before those of subsequent conflicts. Members of the French Résistance get two seats if Charles de Gaulle ever kissed them.

For those who must have a seat at any cost, a few plausible lines are provided.

I was in the Résistance.	J'étais dans la Résistance.	*SHAY-tay dahn lah RAY-zees-tonce.*
As an infant.	Comme nourrisson.	*CUM noo-ree-SOHN.*
I carried messages in my diapers.	Je transportais des messages dans mes langes.	*Shuh TRAHN-spoor-tay day MAY-sahj dahn may LOHN-juh.*
No one dared to search them.	Personne n'a jamais osé les fouiller.	*PAIR-sun nah SHAH-may oh-zay lay FOO-yay.*

But a swine informer turned me in.	Mais un salopard d'indicateur m'a dénoncé.	*May uhn SAL-oh-parr DAN-dee-cah-turr mah DAY-nohn-say.*
I was tortured by the Gestapo.	J'ai été torturé par la Gestapo.	*Shay ay-tay TORE-tij-ray par lah GAY-stop-oh.*
I told them nothing.	Je ne leur ai rien dit.	*Shuh nuh lurr ay RYEN dee.*
I escaped in the bathwater.	Je me suis échappé par l'écoulement de la baignoire.	*Shuh muh swee ZAY-sha-pay par lay-cool-MOHN duh lah ben-warr.*
Give me that seat.	Cédez-moi votre siège.	*SAY-day-mwah voh-truh see-YEHJ.*

RAILWAY ROMANCE

French trains are among the best in the world, but they aren't perfect: one is obliged to share them with the French. Newer trains like the Très Grande Vitesse (TGV, or "Really Big Speed") have an open seating plan, but some of the older trains are still on the tracks. Their cars are divided into compartments that seat six people each.

As every sophisticated traveler knows, there is nothing like a special moment alone with a loved one in a speeding train. The rocking motion of the car, the long, dark tunnels, and the possibility of arrest create an irresistibly romantic atmosphere. The following phrases are meant to help lovers win the private compartment they need to make their train ride really memorable.

Excuse me.	Excusez-moi.	*Ex-KŸ-zay mwah.*
Would you mind clipping my toenails?	Cela vous ennuyerait de me couper les ongles des orteils?	*Suh-lah voo zon-nwee-RAY duh muh coo-pay lay ZON-gluh day-zor-TAY?*
Whoops! Sorry! I didn't mean to spill that coffee on you.	Oh! Pardon! Je n'ai pas fait expès de vous renverser mon café dessus.	*Oh! PAR-dohn! Shuh nay pah fay ex-PRAY duh voo RON-vair-say mohn caf-ay deh-SŸ.*

I really like your moustache.	J'aime beaucoup votre moustache.	*Shem BOH-coo voh-truh moo-STASH.*
It's charming on an older woman.	C'est charmant sur une dame d'un certain âge.	*Say shar-MAHN sür ÿn dahm SAIR-tan ahj.*
You must have been beautiful when you were young.	Vous deviez être très belle quand vous étiez jeune.	*Voo DUH-vyay et-ruh TRAY bell con voo zay-tyay juhn.*
But those front teeth of yours look dead.	Mais vos dents de devant ont l'air fichues.	*May voh DON duh duh-VON on lair FEE-shÿ*

NOTORIOUS SNOUTS, PART I: THE CONCIERGE

Should you rent an apartment in France, your concierge may be a woman who finds her excitement in the intimate details of her tenants' lives. It's best to set the record straight at the beginning.

No, we aren't married.	Non, nous ne sommes pas mariés.	*NOHN, noo nuh somm PAH mah-ree-ay.*
This is my niece/cousin/ daughter/ granddaughter.	C'est ma nièce/cousine/ fille/petite-fille.	*Say mah nee-YES/coo-ZEEN/ FEE/puh-TEET fee.*
No, my wife will not be joining us.	Non, ma femme ne viendra pas nous rejoindre.	*NOHN, mah fahm nuh vyen-drah PAH noo ruh-JWAN-druh.*
Yes, she knows we are here.	Oui, elle sait que nous sommes ici.	*WEE, ell say kuh noo sum zee-SEE.*
No, there is no need for you to telephone her.	Non, vous n'avez pas besoin de lui téléphoner.	*NOHN, voo nah-vay PAH buzz-wan duh lwee TAY-lay-fone-AY.*

NOTORIOUS SNOUTS, PART II: THE RÉCEPTIONISTE

T he female traveler should be aware that the male *réceptioniste* found at a hotel has just two goals in life: making your stay more comfortable and getting a date. He would love to "show you around" the hotel's unoccupied rooms. He whimpers and pleads with a persistence that would embarrass a beagle. He must be dealt with firmly.

You must be joking.	Vous rigolez.	*Voo REE-goh-LAY.*
I never date the help.	Je ne sors jamais avec le personnel.	*Shuh nuh sore SHAM-ay ah-vek luh pair-son-el.*
Yes, I have a boyfriend.	Oui, j'ai un copain.	*WEE, shay uhn coh-pan.*
He's Sicilian.	Il est sicilien.	*Eel ay SEE-seel-yen.*
He likes to step on people's necks.	Il aime bien piétiner la gueule des gens.	*Eel em byen PYAY-tee-nay lah GULL day shon.*
I'm sure he'd be happy to break your legs.	Je suis sûre qu'il serait heureux de vous casser les jambes.	*Shuh swwee SŸR keel ser-ay ur-UH duh voo CASS-ay lay shahmb.*

TINY HOTEL ROOMS OF FRANCE

A weak dollar can turn an already expensive French hotel room into a dramatically over-priced one. Coarse sheets, weird tubular pillows and unidentifiable smells conspire to create a feeling of powerlessness in the tired or inexperienced traveler.

When this sort of emotion reaches the boiling point, it's time to begin complaining.

The bed is big enough for my leg.	Le lit est assez grand pour ma jambe.	*Luh LEE ay tass-ay GRON poor mah shahmb.*
The towel is big enough for my face.	La serviette suffit tout juste à me sécher le visage.	*Lah sair-vyet sÿ-FEE too JŸST ah muh SAY-shay luh vee-SAHJ.*
This is a room for a dwarf.	C'est une chambre pour un nain.	*Sait ÿn SHAHM-bruh poor uhn NAN.*
Every room is like this?	Toutes les chambres sont comme ça?	*TOOT lay shom-bruh sohn cum SAH?*
Are there so many dwarfs in France?	Y a-t-il tant de nains en France?	*Ee ah-teel TAHN duh nan on France?*

THREATENING THE MAID

Maids are the same the world over. They want to get their work done before breakfast. But French people, and French maids in particular, feel morally superior to any person who is unconscious after 7:00 A.M. If you're still in bed at 9:00, honeymoon or no, expect no mercy. And show none.

Since maids don't expect tips, they rarely listen to reason; threats of bodily harm may be required.

Who's there?	Qui est là?	*Kee ay lah?*
Is there a fire?	Il y a le feu?	*Eel ee ah luh FUH?*
You just want to clean the room?	Vous voulez seulement faire le ménage?	*Voo voo-lay SUH-luh-mohn fair luh may-NAHJ?*
Could you come back after dawn?	Revenez après le lever du soleil, voulez-vous?	*RUH-vuh-nay ah-pray luh LUH-vay dÿ so-lay, voo-lay VOO?*
Please do not disturb me again.	Ne me dérangez plus, s'il vous plaît.	*Nuh muh DAY-rahn-shay PLŸ, seel voo play.*
Or I will scratch out your eyes.	Ou je vous arrache les yeux.	*Oo shuh vooz ah-RASH laze yuh.*

TIPPING

Bars and restaurants include a 15 percent *pourboire* (gratuity) in *l'addition* (the bill). this is frustrating for those who like to stiff waiters, but customers who would like to be warmly welcomed upon their return will leave an extra 5 or 10 percent tip, on top of the 15 percent already on the bill.

Most customers leave the coins they receive as change. The waiters then deposit these in their tip cups with the traditional sarcastic saying, *"Royale!"* which is supposed to reflect on a customer's generosity. It would never occur to a French waiter that a tip might reflect on the level of his service.

STIFFING

Theater ushers, even in movie houses, demand tips. Washroom attendants expect some coins but are somewhat less likely to scream if they don't get any. Denying such a person is sometimes possible with the right phrases.

IN THE THEATER:

I insist.	J'insiste.	*SHAHN-sees-tuh.*
Please let us choose our own seats.	Pourriez-vous nous laisser choisir nous-memes nos places?	*POOR-ee-ay-VOO noo less-ay shwah-zeer noo-mem noh PLAHSS?*
I won't tip you.	Votre pourboire passera à l'as.	*Voh-truh poor-BWAR pass-er-AH ah lahss.*
Why don't you get a real job?	Pourquoi ne cherchez-vous pas un vrai boulot?	*Poor-KWAH nuh share-shay-voo PAH uhn VRAY boo-loh?*

IN THE WASHROOM:

I didn't use any of your high-grade toilet paper.	Je n'ai pas touché à votre papier hygiénique super-luxe.	*Shuh nay PAH too-shay ah voh-truh PAH-pyay ee-jyen-eek SŸ-pair-lÿx.*
I didn't wash my hands.	Je ne me suis pas lavé les mains.	*Shuh nuh muh swee PAH lah-vay lay MAN.*
I didn't drip.	Je n'ai pas laissé tomber une seule.	*Shuh nay PAH less-ay TOM-bay ÿn sull.*
I don't owe you a cent.	Je ne vous dois pas un sou.	*Shuh nuh voo dwah PAH uhn SOO.*

FASHION BONDAGE

he Parisian shopping experience is designed to make you feel even fatter and more slovenly than usual. The ensuing panic may cause you to buy more merchandise than you can possibly afford. The only way to avoid financial meltdown is to face the facts: No amount of spending can ever redeem you in the eyes of the slim, effortlessly attractive salespeople.

Oh look! It's the latest style from Madame Macbeth!	Tiens! Le dernier style de Madame Macbeth!	*Tyen! Luh dare-nyay STEEL duh Mah-dahm Mac-BET!*
It's sure to be fashionable for at least another fifteen minutes.	Une mode qui en a encore pour un bon quart d'heure.	*Ÿn mud key on ah on-KOOR poor uhn BUN car durr.*
This would look great.	Cela aurait l'air extraordinaire.	*Suh-lay aw-ray LARE ext-ROAR-dee-NAIR.*
On an alien.	Sur un extra-terrestre.	*Sÿr uhn extra-tair-ESS-truh.*
Maybe.	Du moins, c'est possible.	*Dÿ mwann, say pahss-EE-bluh.*

SIGHTS, SOUNDS, AND SMELLS

It reminds me of an Italian design I saw two years ago.	Cela me fait penser à un modèle italien que j'ai vu il y a deux ans.	*Suh-lah muh fay pon-say ah uhn moh-DELL ee-tal-YEN kuh shay vÿ eel ee ah duh ZON.*
Thank you, no. We're just looking.	Non merci. Nous ne faisons que regarder.	*Nohn mare-SEE. Noo nuh fay-zon kuh ruh-gar-DAY.*

DIETER'S DESIDERATA

Holy Saint Yves, Sacred Designer, Gifted Creator of haute couture, I beseech you to create just one of your heavenly dresses in my size. I have dieted like a jockey for seven years and still cannot fit into your latest creations, Your Blessed Femininity.

Très grand Saint-Yves, Dessinateur Sacré, Créateur Surdoué de la haute couture, je vous prie à genoux de créer pour moi un modèle divin que je puisse porter. Après sept longues années de régime de jockey, je n'arrive toujours pas à entrer dans vos dernières créations, Votre Féminité.

DEMON CHILDREN OF THE EIFFEL TOWER

There are thousands of talented pickpockets in Europe, and most of them are about four feet tall. They usually work in pairs and desist only upon threats of physical violence. Since most of us are reluctant to strike nine-year-old children, a few threatening phrases are supplied here.

Leave us alone.	Fichez-nous la paix.	*FEE-shay NOO lah pay.*
I bought a plastic Eiffel Tower yesterday.	Hier, j'ai acheté une Tour Eiffel en plastique.	*Ee-YAIR, shay ah-shuh-tay ÿn toor ay-FELL on PLAHSS-teek.*
I already own several kilos of brass jewelry.	J'ai déjà plusieurs kilos de bijoux en alliage de laiton.	*Shay day-SHAH PLŸ-zyur kee-loh duh BEE-shoo on ah-lee-yaj duh lay-TOHN.*
I haven't any coins.	Je n'ai pas de petite monnaie.	*Shuh nay PAH duh puh-teet moh-NAY.*
Back off.	De l'air.	*DUH lair.*
I'll break your neck, you little gypsy!	Je te brise le cou, petit gitan!	*Shuh tuh BREEZ luh coo, puh-tee shee-TAHN!*

SIGHTS, SOUNDS, AND SMELLS

Stop, thieves!	Au voleur!	*Oh voh-LURR!*
Police!	Police!	*Poh-LEASE!*
Arrest these children!	Arrêtez ces enfants!	*Ah-ray-TAY say zon-FON!*

PRAYER TO THE DON

Saint Carmine, Prince of Vengeance, Chief of Vendettas, bring a horrible disease to the slimy pickpocket who stole my wallet. In return, I promise never to leave home again without traveler's checks, Your Violence.

Saint-Carmine, Prince de la Vengeance, Patron des Vendettas, transmettez des maladies horribles au pickpocket méprisable qui m'a délesté de mon portefeuille. En reconnaissance de ça, je vous promets de ne plus jamais quitter mon pays sans des chèques de voyage, Votre Violence.

THE MOST GIGANTIC ART MUSEUM ON EARTH

F
rance has found favor with painters since Neanderthal times. Some of the greatest artists, Picasso and Van Gogh among them, left their native lands and moved to France permanently.

Some historians believe that French sunlight has special qualities that bring colors to life for artists. Other experts insist that certain painters had simply bounced too many checks in their own countries.

Whatever the reason for their presence, artists have left millions of paintings and sculptures in France. You won't be able to avoid seeing some of them during your stay.

Which way to the Louvre?	Quelle est la direction pour le Louvre?	*Kel ay lah dee-reck-SYON poor luh LOO-vruh?*
Hey! The line starts back there.	Eh! La queue commence là-bas.	*EH! Lah KUH coh-monce lah bah.*
Who do you think you are? An Italian?	Pour qui vous prenez-vous? Pour un macaroni?	*Poor KEY voo pren-ay voo? Poor uhn mack-ah-roh-NEE?*

SIGHTS, SOUNDS, AND SMELLS

Where is the Winged Victory?	Où est la *Victoire de Samothrace*?	*OO ay lah veek-TWARR duh sah-moh-TRAHSS?*
She got kind of banged-up over the years, didn't she?	Elle a pris un coup de vieux, vous ne trouvez pas?	*El ah pree uhn coo duh VYUH, voo nuh troo-vay PAH?*
Could you direct us to paintings with biblical themes? We've seen only 9,000 so far.	Pourriez-vous nous indiquer des peintures à thèmes bibliques? Nous en avons vu seulement neuf mille jusqu'à présent.	*POOR-ee-ay voo noo IN-dee-kay day pain-TURE ah tem bib-LEEK? News on ah-VAHN vÿ SUHL-mon noof meal shoosk ah pray-SOHN.*
Pardon me, sir.	Excusez-moi, monsieur.	*Ex-KŸ-zay mwah, muh-SYUH.*
We have been here for four days and nights without food or water.	Il y a quatre jours et quatre nuits que nous sommes ici sans nourriture ni la moindre goutte d'eau.	*Eel ee ah KAT-ruh shoor ay KAT-ruh nÿ-ee kuh noo sum zee-SEE sahn noo-ree-TŸR nee lah MWAN-druh goot DOH.*
Could you be our guide to the exit?	Pourriez-vous nous indiquer la sortie?	*POOR-ee-ay-VOO noo ZAN-dee-KAY lah sore-TEE?*

INTELLIGENT COMMENTS ABOUT ART YOU CAN MAKE YOURSELF

A rt museums have been ideal pickup spots for centuries, since they naturally screen out the unwashed.

But simply entering a house of worship such as the Louvre or Pompidou is not enough. Nor is "knowing what one likes" and gawking at it. One must *en mettre plein la vue* (sling bullshit) like a Citroën dealer.

Note: Do not attempt to pronounce van Gogh. It sounds something remotely like "van gohjgkhh." Stick with Vincent, pronounced "van-SAHN."

Notice how the fruit is dramatically outlined in black.	Remarquez comme le fruit est souligné en noir d'une façon dramatique.	*Ruh-mar-KAY cum luh frÿ-ee ay soo-lee-nyay on NWARR dÿn fah-son drah-mah-TEEK.*
Cézanne's little limes almost leap into your mouth.	Les petits citrons verts de Cézanne vous sautent pratiquement dans la bouche.	*Lay puh-tee see-tron VAIR duh Say-ZAHN voo sote prah-teek-mohn dahn lah BOOSH.*

SIGHTS, SOUNDS, AND SMELLS

Have you noticed Monet's bold use of blue here?	Avez-vous remarqué l'audace du bleu dans ce Monet?	*Ah-vay voo RUH-mar-KAY loh-DAHSS dÿ BLUH don suh Moh-NAY?*
The lone water lily signifies the essential loneliness of existence.	Le nénuphar isolé incarne la solitude essentielle de l'existence.	*Luh nay-nÿ-fahr ee-zoh-LAY een-carn lah SOLE-ee-TŸD ess-on-SYEL duh leg-zees-TONCE.*
But the water itself reminds us that passionate lovemaking helps us conquer that loneliness.	Mais l'eau nous rappelle qu'un amour passionné nous aide à conquérir cette solitude.	*May LOH noo rah-pell ken ah-MOOR pah-syon-ay noo-zed ah KON-kay-reer set SOLE-ee-TŸD.*
Let's talk about it over a cup of espresso.	Parlons-en tout en prenant un café express.	*PARL-on-zon toot on pruh-NON uhn KAH-fay ex-PRESS.*

NEGOTIATING THE TOPLESS BEACH

A ttendants at French beaches will insist on payment. In exchange for one's hard-earned euros one may use a chair, an umbrella, and an outdoor shower. Changing rooms are also available, but the French are not *pudiques* (modest).

The attendant may shout and get red in the face when beach-goers refuse to buy any of his services, but there is no law against sitting on your own towel; beaches are public property.

What? I have to pay to sit here?	Quoi? On doit payer pour s'asseoir ici?	*Kwah? On dwah pay-YAY poor sass-warr ee-SEE?*
How much?	Combien?	*COHM-byen?*
Is it more to lie down?	Et si on s'allonge, ça coûte plus cher?	*Ay see on sall-ONSH, sah coot plÿ share?*
I refuse to pay you a cent. Leave me alone.	Je refuse de vous payer un centime. Fichez-moi la paix.	*Shuh ruh-fÿz duh voo pay-ay UHN sahn-teem. FEESH-ay mwah lah pay.*
Go ahead and call the cops, then.	Allez-y, appelez les flics, alors.	*AL-lay-zee, APP-lay lay fleek, ah-lore.*

SIGHTS, SOUNDS, AND SMELLS

Excuse me, miss, but I think you may be burning.	Pardon mademoiselle, mais je crois que vous êtes en train de griller.	*Par-DON mad-mwah-zel, may shuh KWAH kuh voo zet ohn TRAN duh gree-LAY.*
May I lend you some cocoa butter for those?	Me permettez-vous de vous passez cette crème solaire pour ces deux-là?	*Muh PAIR-met-ay VOO duh voo pahss-ay set crem so-lair poor say DUH-lah?*
You've had too much sun today.	Vous êtes restée trop longtemps au soleil aujourd'hui.	*Voo-zet rest-ay TROH lon-tahm oh so-LAY oh-shore-dwee.*
We must get you into a dark room immediately.	On doit vous emmener dans une chambre noire immédiatement.	*On dwah voo zom-mun-AY dahnz ÿn shahm-bruh NWARR ee-MAY-dyat-mohn.*
I also recommend alcoholic beverages.	Je peux vous proposer aussi de l'alcool.	*Shuh puh voo pro-POSE-ay oh-SEE duh LALL-cool.*
Yes. I'm a doctor.	Oui. Je suis médecin.	*WEE. Shuh swee MADE-san.*
Allow me to introduce myself.	Permettez-moi de me présenter.	*Pair-met-ay-MWAH duh muh PRAY-zon-tay.*

CULTIVATING YOUR ATTITUDE PROBLEM

Effective cursing in any language is a matter of attitude, and the French have more attitude than any other species on earth.

In other words, you will likely lose any exchange of curses made on neutral ground. If you feel you must assault someone verbally, try doing it on the phone or from a moving vehicle.

When insulting one person, use the familiar *tu* rather than the formal *vous*. This implies condescension, which the French invented.

| **You bunch of camels!** | Bande de chameaux! | *Bahn duh SHAM-oh!* |

BUREAUCRACY AND CULTURE

You peasants have truffles for brains!	Vous les paysans, vous avez des truffes à la place de cerveau!	*VOO lay pay-ee-ZOHN, vooz ah-vay day TRŸF ah lah plahss duh sair-VOH!*
You make me sick!	Vous me rendez malade!	*Voo muh RON-day mah-LAHD!*
I shit on you, you type of worthless pig!	Je t'emmerde, espèce de porc à la manque!	*Shuh tom-MAIRD, ess-pess duh PORE ah lah mahnk!*
Buzz off, depraved crab louse!	Tire-toi, morpion!	*TEER-TWAH, more-PYON!*
I don't give a shit, defiler of virgins!	Je n'en ai rien à foutre, espèce de dépuceleur de vierges.	*Shuh non ay ryen ah FOO-truh, ess-pess duh DAY-pÿce-lur duh VYAIR-juh.*
Boot-licker!	Lèche-bottes!	*LESH-butt!*
Screw yourself, dog-breath.	Va te faire foutre, fumier à l'haleine de roquet.	*VAH tuh fair FOO-truh, FŸ-myay ah lah-LENN duh roh-KAY.*
I'll see you in hell!	On se reverra en enfer!	*On suh ruh-vair-AH on non-fair!*
Dog-lips!	Ta geule!	*Tah guhll!*
You bug the shit out of me.	Tu me fais shier.	*Tÿ muh fay SHE-ay.*

UNDERSTANDING EUROPEAN BUSINESS HOURS

Those who wonder why they so seldom see French people working may consult the guide below.

	WHAT THEY'RE DOING	**WHAT'S HAPPENING TO YOU**
MORNING		
8:00	Black coffee, lots of sugar. Looks like hot tar.	Attempt to sleep foiled by maid. Again.
9:00	Late for work. Coffee coursing through veins. Drive like mad.	Step out of hotel, almost killed by speeding motorist.
10:00	Chat on phone. Quasi-business purpose for conversation.	Try to change money, but mob overwhelms lone clerk.
11:00	Make lunch plans.	Shopkeeper on phone. Fail to get his attention.
AFTERNOON		
12:00	Drop by a friend's office.	Attempt to contact local travel agent. She isn't in.
1:00	Late for lunch. Drive like hell.	Ride in taxi, almost killed on way to museum.

BUREAUCRACY AND CULTURE

2:00	Lunch with entire family.	Museum closed.
3:00	Speak with friends on telephone, plan evening.	Begin drinking.
4:00	More coffee.	Return to bank. Ready to kill line jumpers.

EVENING

5:00	Average 180 kph on drive to office.	Huge crowd at travel agency. Chuckle good-naturedly.
6:00	Look up from phone call. Make hand motion: *"Un moment."*	Obtain euros and tickets. Finally. Head back to café.
7:00	Race home. Change clothes. Argue with spouse/children.	Seated in café, almost killed by speeding car.
8:00	Race to meet lover. Almost killed by speeding vehicle.	Decide to "borrow" big Citroën. Go for joyride.
10:00	Quiet dinner at home.	At dinner, restaurant seems full of grotesque tourists.

LATE EVENING

12:00	Retire to separate bedroom.	Unable to find taxi.
1:00	Well-earned sleep.	Eventually find hotel. Greet maids beginning their day's work.

WAITING FOR GODOT'S TELEGRAM

Many French people rely on the post office (PTT) for telephones, telegrams, even checking accounts. One can find stamps at the PTT, of course, but these are for sale in cafés and tobacco shops as well. Postal workers are not known for being helpful; you'll get more sympathy from raw oysters.

The French will loudly defend their postal service as being far superior to the American version. That, of course, isn't much of a boast.

I would like to send this airmail to California.	Je voudrais envoyer cette lettre par avion en Californie.	*Shuh voo-DRAY on-vwah-YAY set LET-ruh par ah-VYON on cal-ee-for-NEE.*
How much will that cost?	Combien cela va-t-il me coûter?	*Com-BYEN suh-lah vah-teel muh COO-tay?*
Look at all your record books! How quaint.	Regardez tous ces livres! Comme vous êtes vieux jeu.	*RUH-gar-DAY too say LEE-vruh! Cum voo zet vyuh shuh.*
Do you think it will arrive in time for Christmas?	Pensez-vous que la lettre arrivera à temps pour Noël?	*PONCE-ay voo kuh lah LET-ruh ah-REEV-uh-rah ah tohmp poor noh-EL?*

No? In time for Easter, then?	Non? Pour Pâques, alors?	*Nohn? Poor PAK, ah-LORE?*
Maybe his/her great-grandchildren will receive it before dying of old age.	Peut-être ses arrières-petits-enfants la recevront-ils avant de mourir de vieillesse.	*Puh-TET-ruh saze AR-ee-YAIR puh-teez on-FON lah RUH-suh-vron-TEEL ah-VONT duh moo-REER duh vyay-ESS.*
No need to apologize.	Ne vous excusez pas.	*Nuh vooz ex-CŸ-zay pah.*
Thank you for being so gracious.	Merci de votre amabilité.	*Mare-SEE duh voh-truh AM-ah-bee-lee-tay.*
Have you been checked for rabies recently?	Est-ce-que vous avez été examiné pour la rage récemment?	*Ess-kuh vooz ah-vay ay-tay ex-am-ee-nay poor lah RAHJ ray-sah-mahn?*
Excuse me, but have you a porcupine stuck up your rear end?	Pardonnez-moi, mais avez-vous un porc-épic coincé entre les fesses?	*PAR-don-ay-mwah, may ah-vay-voo uhn PORK-ay-pick kwan-say on-truh lay FESS?*
Same to you and your grandmother.	La même chose à vous et à votre grand-mère.	*Lah mem shose ah VOO ay ah voh-truh gron-MAIR.*

NO BAD WAITERS

Many restaurant employees, from *saucier* to *sommelier*, bear emotional scars from past experiences serving foreigners. French waiters, especially those in Paris, are not known for their friendly demeanor, even towards other Frenchmen. And once they hear you speaking English, they cannot help but assume that you are a Stone Age pagan. When a waiter is suffering from such a prejudice, his manners may slip to reveal the beast beneath the tuxedo. Keep him in line with a few choice phrases.

Sir, is it true that you're ashamed of your menu?	Monsieur, est-ce vrai que vous avez honte de votre menu?	*Muh-SYUH, ess VRAY kuh vooz ah-vay ONT duh voh-truh men-Ÿ?*
Perhaps you would show us a copy, then.	Pourriez-vous nous en faire voir un exemplaire, alors.	*Poor-ee-ay voo noo-zon fare VWARR uhn ex-ohm-plair, ah-LORE.*
Could we have a pitcher of water?	Pourrait-on avoir une carafe d'eau?	*Poo-rate-on ah-VWARR ÿn kah-rahf DOH?*
Tap water, please. With ice.	De l'eau du robinet, s'il vous plaît. Avec des glaçons.	*Duh loh dÿ ROH-bee-nay, seel voo play. Ah-vek day GLAH-son.*

It's the hard, cold stuff the Eskimos like so much.	Ce truc dur et froid que les Esquimaux aiment tellement.	*Suh trÿk DŸR ay FWAH kuh laze ESS-kee-moh EM tel-luh-mahn.*
If you continue to take that attitude, I swear I'll smother my soufflé in ketchup.	Si vous continuez à vous conduire comme ça, je jure de noyer mon soufflé dans du ketchup.	*See voo con-tin-ÿ-ay ah voo con-DWEER cum sah, shuh SHOOR duh NWAH-yay mohn soo-FLAY don dÿ ket-SHUP.*
I'm afraid it's now past dinnertime.	J'ai bien peur que l'heure du dîner ne soit passée.	*Shay byen PUR kuh LUR dÿ dee-NAY nuh swah POSS-ay.*
Please change my order to a Continental breakfast.	Veuillez changer ma commande pour un petit déjeuner à la française.	*Vuh-yay SHON-shay mah com-MAHND poor uhn puh-TEE day-shuh-nay ah lah fron-SEZ.*
Wake me when it arrives.	Réveillez-moi quand il arrivera.	*RUH-vay-ay mwah con teel ah-REE-vuh-rah.*

ORGANS YOU MAY WISH TO AVOID EATING

T he French are resourceful when it comes to consuming whatever they pull out of the water, the ground, and the woods. Travelers who prefer to remain unfamiliar with the appearance, texture, and flavor of these creatures and their parts may need some excuses to turn down the waiter's unwelcome suggestions.

I had blackbird pie for lunch.	J'ai mangé du pâté de merle pour aux déjeuner.	*Shay MON-shay dÿ PAT-ay duh MAIRL poor oh DAY-shun-ay.*
I'm trying to cut down on liver from anemic calves.	J'essaie de restreindre ma consommation de foie de veau.	*Shess-ay duh ress-tran-druh mah con-som-ah-SYON duh FWAH duh voh.*
I'm allergic to calf's marrow soup.	Je suis allergique au potage à la moelle de veau.	*Shuh swee ZAL-air-jeek oh POH-tahj ah lah MWAHL duh voh.*
I don't think thyroid glands would go well with my appetizer.	Je ne pense pas que les ris de veau se marient bien avec mon hors-d'oeuvre.	*Shuh nuh ponce pah kuh luh REE duh voh suh MAH-ree byen ah-VEK mohn or-DUH-vruh.*

Pig's blood sausage is just too rich for me.	Le boudin noir est un peu trop lourd à mon goût.	*Luh boo-dan NWAR ay tuhn puh troh LOOR ah mohn goo.*
I believe a stew of goose organs and goose blood is out of season.	Je ne pense pas que ce soit la saison pour du civet de tripes d'oie au sang.	*Shuh ne ponce pah kuh suh swah lah SAY-zohn poor dÿ SEE-vay duh TREEP dwah oh sohn.*
I'm saving stew of blood-sucking eels for a very special occasion.	Je réserve la lamproie à la bordelaise pour une occasion spéciale.	*Shuh ray-zerv lah lom-pwah ah lah bord-uh-LEZ poor ÿn oh-caz-yohn SPAY-syal.*
Tonight I'm in the mood for filet of sole with French fries.	C soir j'ai envie d'un filet de sole avec des frites.	*Suh SWAR shay on-vee duhn FEE-lay duh SOLE ah-vek day FREET.*

WINE TALK OF THE SOPHISTICATES

Of all the products of France, wine is one of the most admired by Frenchmen and foreigners alike. Talking knowledgeably about wine marks the true sophisticate.

The wine has great legs.	Ce vin a de la jambe.	*Suh VAN ah duh lah shom-buh.*
Yes, but its buttocks are wrinkled.	Oui, mais il a la fesse fripée.	*WEE, may eel ah lah FESS free-pay.*
The Haut-Médoc tries to grease the palate but scratches instead.	Ce Haut-Médoc essaie de me graisser le palais mais n'arrive qu'à l'écorcher.	*Suh OH-may-DUK ESS-ay duh muh GRESS-ay luh pah-LAY may nah-reev kah LAY-cor-shay.*
This Beaucastel rouge is plump and amusing.	Ce Beaucastel rouge est calin et bien charnu.	*Suh BOH-cass-tel roo jhay CAH-lan ay BYEN shar-nÿ.*
What a delightful aroma of hazelnuts and sardines!	Quel superbe bouquet de noisettes et de sardines!	*Kell sÿ-PAIR-buh bouquet duh NWAH-zet ay duh sar-DEEN!*

The Armagnac was clever but shy.	L'Armagnac était futé mais trop discret.	*LAR-mah-nyak ay-tay foo-TAY may TROH dees-cray.*
The Vouvray is pimply but forthright.	Le Vouvray a des aspérités mais il est sincère.	*Luh voo-VRAY ah day ZAH-spare-ee-tay may eel AY san-sair.*
The Château Montrose is an ungrateful bitch.	Le Château Montrose est une roulure sans gratitude.	*Luh SHA-toh mohn-rose ay tijn roo-LŸR sohn grah-tee-TŸD.*

This Sauternes has socialist tendencies.	Ce Sauternes a des tendances socialistes.	*Suh Saw-TAIRN ah day ton-DONCE soh-syah-leest.*
Romanée-Conti is forever a sublime ferret in my underpants.	Le Romanée-Conti restera à jamais un sublime rat de cave dans mon caleçon.	*Luh ROH-mah-nay cohn-TEE rest-uh-rah ah shah-may uhn sÿj-bleem RAH duh cahv dahn mohn CAL-sohn.*

DOMINATING THE DISCO

French people like to go to the disco. The trouble is, they can't dance. Because they are about as funky as the Japanese, the French love to watch Americans go wild. This is one of the two things Frenchmen admire about the United States.

The other is California.

I learned to dance in L.A.	J'ai appris à danser à Los Angeles.	*Shay ah-PREE ah DON-say ah loss AN-jeh-less.*
I live in San Francisco.	J'habite à San Francisco.	*Shah-BEET ah SAHN Frahn-see-skoh.*
Marin County, actually. You know California?	Le Marin County, en fait. Vous connaissez la Californie?	*Luh MAH-ran con-TEE, on fet. Voo con-ay-SAY lah cal-ee-for-NEE?*
Of course, I have a house in Malibu as well.	Bien sûr, j'ai également une maison à Malibu.	*Byen SŸR, shay ay-gal-MAHN ÿn may-ZOHN ah mal-ee-BOO.*
Sometimes I need to be near my movie studios.	J'ai parfois besoin d'être près de mes studios de cinéma.	*Shay par-FWAH buzz-WAN det-ruh PRAY duh may stÿ-dyoh duh see-nay-MAH.*

Aren't you an actor/actress?	Vous êtes acteur/actrice?	*Voo-zet ak-TUR/ ak-TREECE?*
You really should have a screen test.	Vous devriez vraiment faire un essai à l'écran.	*Voo dev-ree-ay VRAY-maahn fair uhn ess-ay ah lay CRAHN.*
This evening, perhaps?	Ce soir, peut-être?	*Suh SWARR, puh tet-ruh?*
Let's split, babe.	On se tire, poupée.	*On suh TEER, poo-pay.*

EXOTIC DRINKS OF THE FRENCH NIGHTCLUB

Once they leave the dinner table, the French seem to forget about their *vins* and *apéritifs*, undoubtedly the finest in the world. By the time nightclubbers reach their destination, they seem to have only one thing in mind: getting ripped.

One needs four words to encompass a French disco's entire beverage selection: scotch, vodka, Coke *(koh-KAH)*, and Banga *(ban-GAH)*, a type of orange soda. These can be drunk in any combination without offending anyone.

CAFÉ ETIQUETTE

No matter how drunk you get:

- Do not sing, even if you suddenly realize how to speak French.
- Do not make political speeches or announcements.
- Do not slap strangers on the back.
- Do not force-feed *apéritifs* to strangers or their dogs.

EXISTENTIALISM AND OTHER BULL

France has produced many important philosophers for two reasons: (1) the French love to sit in cafés and say things; and (2) saying intelligent things is the best way to seduce innocent young graduate students.

To continue the tradition of these innovative playboys, travelers should sprinkle their conversation with the following classics.

JEAN-PAUL SARTRE:

I hate people who say they are existentialists.	Je haïs les gens qui se disent existentialistes.	*Shuh hay-ee lay shon key suh DEEZ EGG-zee-STON-shal-EAST.*

CAFÉS AND NIGHTLIFE

RENÉ DESCARTES:

I think in French; therefore I am.	Je pense en français; donc je suis.	*Shuh ponce on fron-SAY: donk shuh swee.*
I think; therefore I am French.	Je pense; donc je suis français.	*Shuh ponce; donk shuh swee fron-SAY.*

FRED KIERKEGAARD:

The less I think, the more I am.	Moins je pense, plus j'existe.	*Mwann shuh ponce, plÿ SHEG-zeest.*
Passion is the hallmark of existence, my little cabbage.	La passion est la garantie de l'existence, mon petit chou.	*Lah PASS-yon ay lah GARE-ahn-TEE duh LEGG-zeest-AHNCE, mon puh-TEE shoe.*

JACQUES COUSTEAU:

Zuh most graceful creatures can also be zuh deadliest.	Les créatures les plus gracieuses peuvent être aussi les plus mortelles.	*Lay CRAY-ah-ture lay plÿ GRAH-see-YUZ puhv ET-ruh oh-SEE lay plÿ more-TELL.*
In zuh sea, zaire ees no cruelty, only zuh struggle to survive.	Dans la mer il n'y a pas de cruauté, mais seulement l'angoisse de survivre.	*Dahn lah maire eel nyah pah duh CRŸ-oh-TAY, may suh-luh-mahn lang-WASS duh sÿr-VEEV-ruh.*

BANISHING SHRIMPS

Frenchmen are often less robust than their American counterparts. Their *savoir-faire* tends to make up for it; their accents alone are enough to make many American women melt. But women who'd like to hold out for somebody at least an inch taller than they are will need a few killing phrases to get rid of diminutive hangers-on.

Excuse me. I didn't see you down there.	Oh pardon. Je ne vous avais pas vu là, tout en bas.	*Oh PAR-dohn. Shuh nuh voo zah-vay pah VŸ lah, TOO tohn bah.*
Stand up!	Debout!	*DUH-boo!*
Have you lost your mommy?	Tu as perdu ta maman?	*Tÿ ah pair-DŸ tah mah-mahn?*
Wait a sec. You're a jockey, right?	Attendez un peu. Vous êtes jockey, hein?	*AT-on-day uhn puh. Voo-zet show-KAY, ehn?*
No! I know! You're a movie star!	Non! J'y suis! Vous êtes une vedette de cinéma.	*Nohn! SHEE swee! Voo zet ÿn VUH-dett duh see-nay-MAH.*
You played alongside Snow White, right?	Vous avez joué dans Blanche Neige, pas vrai?	*Voo zah-vay shew-ay dohn blonsh-NEHJ, pah VRAY?*

I'm sure women must love you.	Je suis sûr que les femmes vous adorent.	*Shuh swee SŸR kuh lay fahm voo ZAH-door.*
At least those who like to have their kneecaps licked.	Enfin, celles qui aiment se faire bouffer les rotules.	*On-FANN, sell kee em suh fair BOO-fay lay roh-tÿl.*

FAVORITE PET NAMES

The following French terms of endearment are authentic. It is better to use them than to translate your personal favorites. "My sweet potato pie," for example, doesn't work. Yams are not widely admired in France.

My cabbage.	***Mon chou.***	*Mohn shoe.*
My chicken.	***Ma poulette/ mon pooulet.***	*Mah POO-lett/ mohn POO-lay.*
My hen.	***Ma cocotte.***	*Mah coh-CUT.*
My dove.	***Ma tourterelle.***	*Mah TOOR-tuh-rell.*
My kitten.	***Mon minet.***	*Mohn MEE-nay.*
My flea.	***Ma puce.***	*Mah pÿs.*

CAFÉS AND NIGHTLIFE

THE WORDS OF LOVE

Any man hoping to offer serious romantic competition in Europe must exaggerate. There is a certain inflation inherent in French "lines" because they've been in use for thousands of years. Phrases we consider original and cunning, such as "What a pretty name," and "Do you come here often?" lost their power back in the thirteenth century.

You are one fabulous babe.	Vous êtes une super nana.	*Voo zet ÿn SOO-pair nah-nah.*
You are an angel come to earth.	Vous êtes un ange descendu sur terre.	*Voo zet uh NONJ day-sohn-DŸ sÿr tair.*
Your eyes are as blue as the sea of my love for you is large.	Vos yeux sont aussi bleus que l'océan de mon amour pour vous est grand.	*Voh zyuh sohn toh-see BLUH kuh LOH-say-ahn duh mohn ah-MOOR poor voo ay grahn.*
I don't care if the sun never rises again, so long as you love me.	Cela m'est bien égal que le soleil ne se lève plus, si seulement vous m'aimez.	*Suh-lah may byen nay-GAL kuh luh so-LAY nuh suh lev plÿ, see suh-luh-mohn voo MAY-may.*

I am only an earthworm without you.	Sans vous je ne suis qu'un ver de terre.	*Sahn VOO shuh nuh swee kuhn VAIR duh tair.*
Come away with me on my yacht, my little cabbage.	Enfuyons nous ensemble sur mon yacht, mon petit chou.	*ON-fwee-yon noo on-SOM-bluh sÿr mon YUT, mohn puh-tee SHOE.*
And what is your name, my jewel of thirty-six carats?	Comment vous appelez-vous, mon bijou de trente-six carats?	*COM-on voo ZAP-lay voo, mohn BEE-shoo duh tron-SEECE cah-rah?*
Ah! Your husband!/ My wife!	Ciel! Votre mari!/ Ma femme!	*See-YELL! Voh-truh MAH-ree/ Mah FAHM!*
Au revoir.	Au revoir.	*Oh ruh-VWARR.*

YOUR EMERGENCY CONFESSION

When far from home, some people do things they later regret. Luckily for them, France is still a Catholic country. The French see no need to live with their guilt; they simply confess. For those who wish to engage in this clever practice, the following phrases may be helpful.

Forgive me, Father, for I have sinned.	Pardonnez-moi, mon Père, car j'ai péché.	*PAR-donn-ay-MWAH, mohn PAIR, car j'ai shay PAY-shay.*
It has been six hours/days/ weeks/months/ years since my last confession.	Cela fait six heures/jours/sem- aines/mois/ans que je ne me suis pas confessé(e).	*Suh-lah fay SEE zuhr/shoor/suh- MEN/mwah/on kuh shuh nuh muh swee pah CON-fay-say.*
I picked up a girl/boy in a fine restaurant.	J'ai dragué une fille/un garçon dans un restaurant vraiment bien.	*Shay DRAH-gay ün fee/uhn gar-SOHN dahn zuhn res-toh- rohn VRAY-mahn byen.*
Yes, I realize how serious that is.	Oui, oui, je sais que c'est très grave.	*Wee, wee, shuh SAY kuh say tray grahv.*

But I also drank a Gewürtztraminer with roasted duck.	Mais j'ai bu aussi du Gewürtztraminer avec du canard rôti.	*May shay bÿ oh-SEE dÿ guh-VAIRTS-trah-MEAN-er ah-vek dÿ can-ARR roh-TEE.*
Are you choking, Father?	Vous suffoquez, mon Père?	*Voo sÿ-foh-KAY, mohn pair?*
Wait, there's more. I made love to a Belgian.	Attendez, ce n'est pas tout. J'ai couché avec un/une belge.	*Ah-TOHN-day, suh NAY pah too. Shay coo-SHAY ah-vek uhn/ÿn belge.*
Burning at the stake does seem a little severe.	Brûler au bûcher me semble un peu dur.	*Brÿ-lay oh Bÿÿÿÿÿÿÿÿÿÿÿÿÿÿÿÿÿÿÿÿÿÿÿÿÿÿÿÿÿÿÿ-shay muh somm-bluh uhn puh DÿR.*
How abut a few thousand "Our Fathers" instead?	Que pensez-vous de quelques milliers de "Notre Père"?	*Kuh PONN-say voo duh kell-kuh mee-lee-yay duh noh-truh PAIR?*
Thank you, Father. Oh, one more thing.	Merci, mon Père. Oh, un moment.	*Mare-SEE, mohn pair. Oh, uhn moh-MOHN.*
Can you recommend a good restaurant?	Vous ne connaîtriez pas un bon petit restaurant?	*Voo nuh con-ay-tree-ay PAH uhn bohn puh-tee res-toh-ROHN?*

THE MODEL GUEST

YOUR FIRST RURAL EXPERIENCE

E very year, a few lucky foreigners get the chance to stay on a farm with a French family. They should be ready for hard work and delicious home-cooked meals. A typical day may include early rising, heavy lifting, and eye-watering odors. Getting along with the family should be no problem if you memorize a few key phrases.

I'm afraid I don't know much about milking/slaughtering cows.	Je crains ne pas bien m'y connaître dans la traite des vaches/l'abattage du bétail.	*Shuh cran nuh pah mee con-ET-ruh dahn lah tret day vahsh/lah-bah-TASH dÿ bay-TIE.*
You mean you shovel this much every day?	Vous voulez dire que vous bêchez tout ça chaque jour?	*Voo voo-lay DEER kuh voo bay-shay too sah shack SHOOR?*
We're going to kill this little calf? In honor of my visit?	On va tuer ce petit veau? En mon honneur?	*Ohn vah TŸ-ay suh puh-tee VOH? On mohn noh-NUR?*
Actually, I prefer my veal on the hoof.	Pour tout vous avouer, je préfère le veau sur pied.	*Poor too voo zah-voo-AY, shuh pray-FAIR luh VOH sÿr PYAY.*

THE INEVITABLE THANK-YOU LETTER

Experienced travelers always write *un billet de remerciments* (a thank-you note) to a kind host or hostess, and a postcard or two to each interesting person they have met on a trip. This ensures a warm welcome upon return to France, and often leads to kind invitations, the sort that can help one avoid those bothersome restaurant and hotel bills. The following are a few common phrases used in letter writing.

Dear Pierre/ **Dear Monique,**	Cher Pierre/ Chère Monique,
Thank you for the **unforgettable day/** **evening/weekend.**	Je tiens à vous remercier pour cette journée/cette soireé/ce week-end inoubliable.
I'll never see Paris the **same way again.**	Je ne verrai plus jamais Paris avec les mêmes yeux.
You've opened up a **whole new world for me.**	Vous m'avez fait découvrir un monde entièrement nouveau.
I've got a terrible rash **that won't go away.**	J'ai attrapé une urticaire dont je n'arrive pas à me guérir.

(continued)

THE MODEL GUEST

But I must say your cooking was magnificent.	Mais je dois reconnaître que votre cuisine était superbe.
The carbon duck was particularly fine.	Le canard calciné était vraiment extraordinaire.
As was the sly, aggressive Margaux.	De même que le Margaux, astringent et un peu traître.
The "dessert" you had planned was also delicious.	Le "dessert" que vous aviez prévu était également délicieux.
My only regret is that it was all over so quickly.	Mon seul regret est d'en avoir à peine vu la couleur.
I look forward to seeing you again someday.	J'espère avoir le plaisir de vous revoir un jour.
Perhaps by then one of us will be divorced/ bilingual.	Peut-être qu'à ce moment là, l'un de nous deux sera-t-il divorcé/bilingue.
Hope your rash is every bit as virulent as mine.	J'espère que votre éruption est aussi virulente que la mienne.
Yours truly, (Your name)	Veuillez agréer l'assurance de mon souvenir ému, (Your name)

Wicked
GERMAN

Natürlich hätte ich gerne ein Stück von Ihrem Strudel.

Naturally, I would enjoy a piece of your strudel.

*Nah-TEWR-leekh heh-teh eekh GAIR-neh ein SHTEWK
fohn EE-rem SHTROO-dell.*

CONTENTS

SIGHTSEEING

ENTERTAINMENT & NIGHTLIFE

BUSINESS

GET A GRIP ON GERMAN

Germany is one of the few countries in continental Europe where a typical American can blend in. Once you remove the sneakers and baseball cap, all you need are odd shoes and a dated haircut.

Germans and Americans have a great deal in common, including genes, a car culture, substantial girth, and a built-in domineering attitude. While that bossy nature has gotten us all into a lot to trouble over the years, it does allow us to understand each other well, regardless of the language barrier.

To be sure, the German and English languages have intermingled over the centuries, thanks to the congress of monarchs, vast German immigration and informative television programs such as *Hogan's Heroes*.

The two languages are so similar that we can grasp many German phrases upon first hearing. Some, including *ersatz*, *kitsch* and *dreck*, have entered English in their original form.

Others are understandable despite spelling differences, such as *bringen* (bring), *Blume* (flower), *dumm* (intellectually challenged), and *Pudel* (poodle).

Travelers who learn a few words will be able to decipher dozens of common phrases. Once you know that *aus* means "out," for example, you can guess the meaning of *aushängen, ausbomben* and *ausflippen.**

But sensing what Germans mean is not enough; you must be ready to counter with sharp ripostes. These issue from the back of the throat between the points of gargle and gag. A loud, stern voice and a couple of tablespoons of saliva add emphasis.

Armed with these phrases, a rigid attitude and a haughty bearing, you will win the battles fought by travelers since Romans first crossed the Alps. Or at least vent your frustrations.

Viel Glück.

* hang out, bomb out, flip out

PRONUNCIATION GUIDE

erman pronunciation is every bit as precise as a Hasselblad camera or a Glock automatic pistol. Even if our mouths were made of the finest Ruhr Valley steel, we foreigners could never achieve perfect pronunciation. Bettering our fellow tourists' pronunciation is easy, however, if we follow these simple rules.

Vowel sounds are absolutely distinct: a = "ah," e = "ay," i = "ee," o = "oh," u = "oo" and $ü$ = "euyuue." The $ü$ is an "eee" sound made with the lips protruding as if to suck foam from an overflowing stein.

Early Germans, known as Neanderthals, discovered two special "ch" sounds. The hard "ch" is formed after the vowels a, o, u, and au, furball-like at the back of the throat. This hard "ch" does not exist in English but has survived in Hebrew.

The soft "ch," even more difficult, hisses further forward in the mouth and is formed after the vowels e, i, ä, ü, ie, ei, äu, eu. As the fat part of the tongue nears the palate, the hissing begins.

Make these sounds each day for exactly two hours before breakfast and exactly two hours after dinner. As your back begins to straighten and your facial muscles freeze up, you'll begin to look and feel more German. You've captured the essence of the Teutonic spirit, and doing that is the secret to learning any language.

TALK IN THE PROVINCES

German scholars believe that spoken German includes dialects from three basic categories: High, Low, and *Ausländisch.*

Dutch and Flemish are said to to be forms of Low German. Yiddish derives from High German while French, Italian, Polish, Russian and Greek are all dialects from the third category: *Ausländisch.* Apparently the German "Uberlanguage" was spread across the continent by roving tribes of stern German schoolteachers.

The university, or High, German used in this book makes it useful all over Germany, Austria and Switzerland, allowing readers to subdue wrathful Goths wherever they are found.

LINGUISTIC DISCLAIMER AND EXCULPATORY PROTESTATION

The author and his translators, agents, publisher, editors, attorneys, heirs, personal friends and armed bodyguards hereby throttle, pummel and utterly humiliate any claim, tort or tart arising from the use or misuse of words, phrases, concepts, or attitudes contained herein.

HOTEL EXISTENCE

A lmost all Germans—including hotel staff—share an interest in philosophy. Sprinkling your complaints with quotes from native thinkers will enhance your prestige around the *Gasthaus* much more than any threat or gold card possibly could.

IMMANUEL KANT (1724–1804)

Time and Space exist only in our minds.	Zeit und Raum existieren nur in unseren Köpfen.	*TSEIT oont ROWM ai-xis-TEE-ren noor in OON-zay-ren KUHP-fen.*
Where the hell is room service?	Wo zum Teufel bleibt der Zimmerservice?	*VOH tsoom TOY-fel bleibt dair TSIM-mair-SURH-vees?*

ARTHUR SCHOPENHAUER (1788–1860)

No matter how deeply we investigate, we can never reach anything except images and names.	Wie immer man auch forschen mag: so gewinnt man nichts als Bilder und Namen.	*Vee EEM-mair mahn owkh FOHR-shen makh: zoh gay-VEENNT mahn NEEKHTS ahls BEEL-dair oont NAH-men.*
Although I do smell a foul odor in the bathroom area.	Obwohl ich einen faulen Geruch um das Badezimmer herum rieche.	*Ohp-vohl eekh EI-nen FOW-len gay-ROOKH oom dahs BAH-deh-TSIM-mer hair-OOM REE-kheh.*

ACCOMMODATION, FOOD AND DRINK

FRIEDRICH NIETZSCHE (1844–1900)

I have plumbed the depths in the soul of the highest man.	Ich habe die Tiefen in der Seele des höchsten Menschen ergründet.	*Eekh-HAH-beh dee TEE-fen in dair ZAY-leh dess HUHKH-sten MEN-shen air-GREWN-deht.*
Now fetch me some sedatives.	Nun holen Sie mir ein Beruhigungsmittel.	*Noon HOH-len zee meer ein bay-ROO-ee-goon(g)z MEET-tel.*

GOTTFRIED WILHELM LEIBNIZ (1646–1716)

There is no chaos or confusion.	Es gibt kein Chaos, keine Verwirrung.	*Ess geebt kein KAH-ohs, KEI-neh fair-VEER-roon(g).*
It only looks that way to the maid.	Der Magd ersheint es nur so.	*Dair MAHKT air-SHEINT ess noor ZOH.*

HISTORY OF BEER

Germans make many things well, and beer is among their greatest achievements. Its exact origins have been lost among thousands of groggy mornings and sledgehammer headaches, but this is what scholars now believe about beer's history.

c. 20,000 B.C.	Og of Url eats a handful of yeast with his gruel and water. He is hailed as the Father of Beer and Life of the Party at his funeral the next day.
c. 11,000 B.C.	Herman of Villendorf drinks 12 steins of lager in 1.79 seconds, breaking the world record. His subsequent belch also sets a record, killing 28.
c. 6000 B.C.	Henrik the Effete, the first beer connoisseur, invents the sip. He is banished to France.
c. 1516 B.C.	The German Purity Law is written to protect the quality of beer. Anyone caught drinking Coors is spanked to death by a 300-pound barmaid.

ACCOMMODATION, FOOD AND DRINK

500 A.D.	Huns descend on Germany looking for riches, virgins, pretzels and a genuine fire-brewed beer with no aftertaste.
501-1870	Hun celebration.
1871	Otto von Bismarck settles Germany's major dispute and unites the nation with his decree on Dinkel Acker Light: Tastes great *and* less filling.
1961	Berlin Wall erected. East German government bans every brand of beer except Harnburgh. The party appears to be over.
1990	East Germans, hearing rumors about the classic taste of ice-cold Spaten, knock down the Berlin Wall, party nonstop and run up a six-billion-dollar bar tab.
2005	Low-carb diet craze hits the Western world. German beer drinkers fail to notice.

BEER-HALL SMALL TALK

Biergärten or *Hofbräuhäuser* (beer halls) can be as big and noisy as gyms. When strangers sit down and attempt to engage you in conversation use one or more of these all-purpose rejoinders.

Cheers/health/ Fatherland!	Prost/Gesundheit/ Vaterland!	*Prohst/Ge-ZOONT- height/FAH-tair- lahnd!*
Here's mud/spit in your eye!	Da ist Dreck/Spucke in Ihrem Auge!	*Dah isst DRAIK/SHPOOK-uh een EE-ren OW-geh!*
I agree completely!	Ganz meine Meinung!	*GAHNTS mei-neh MEI-noong!*
But that happens to be my wife/husband!	Aber das ist nur meine Frau/mein Mann!	*AH-bair DAHS ist noor mei-neh FROW/mein MAHN!*
Now you've crossed the line, you bag of schnitzel!	Nun haben Sie aber die Grenze überschritten, Sie Schnitzelrancher!	*Noon HAH-ben zee AH-bair dee GREN-tseh EW-bair- SHRIT-ten, zee SHNIT-sel-RAN-chur!*
Taste knucklewurst!	Riecht Knöchelwurst!	*Reecht NOOKL- worst!*

BEER CONNOISSEURSHIP

Beer is to Germans what wine is to the French. Impress your hosts by speaking knowingly about beer in a loud, authoritative voice.

This Malz has a strong oak flavor with a faint almond backwash.	Dieses Malzbier hat einen starken Eichengeschmack und beim Aufstoßen schmeckt es leicht nach Mandeln.	*DEE-zess MAHLTS-beer haht ein-en SHTAHR-ken EI-khen-ge-SHMAHK oont beim OWF-shtohs-sen shmehkt ess leikht nahkh MAHN-deln.*

The Hefe-Weizen has big feet and a small head.	Wiezenbier hat große Füße und einen kleinen Kopf.	*VEI-tsayn-beer haht GROH-seh FEW-seh oont ei-nen KLEI-nen KOHPF.*
You can taste eggs beneath the vigorous schnauzer.	Sie können Eier unter diesem vitalen Schnauzer schmecken.	*Zee kuhn-nen EI-er oon-tair dee-zehm vee-TAHL-en SHNOW-tser shmek-ken.*

(continued)

ACCOMMODATION, FOOD AND DRINK

The tanned, curvaceous Rauchbier displays a fine set of bubbles.	Das gebräunte, kurvenreiche Rauchbier zeigt einen feinen Satz von Blasen.	*Dahs geh-BROIN-teh, KOOR-vehn-rei-kheh ROWKH-beer tseikt ei-nen FEI-nen ZAHTS fohn BLAH-zehn.*
Your Doppelbock gives off a bold aroma of sweat and glue.	Ihr Doppelbock riecht stark nach Schweiß und Kleister.	*Eehr DOHP-payl-bohk reekht SHTAHRK nahkh SCHVEISS oont KLEI-ster.*
The aftertaste is reminiscent of ball bearings.	Der Nachgeschmack erinnert an Kugellager	*Dair NAHKH-geh-shmahck air-EEN-nairt ahn KOO-gail-LAH-ger.*
My eyeballs hurt after just one glass.	Meine Augäpfel schmerzen nach nur einem Glas.	*MEI-neh OWG-aip-fell SHMAIR-tsen nahkh noor EI-nehm glahs.*
My stomach feels like an old woodchuck.	Mein Magen fühlt sich an wie ein altes Waldmurmeltier.	*Mein MAH-gen fewlt seekh ahn vee ein AHL-tess VAHLT-moor-mell-teer.*
Another round? Certainly!	Noch eine Runde? Klar!	*NOHKH ei-neh ROON-deh? Klahr!*

A VISIT TO BLITZ

Just as Eskimos are said to have a hundred words for snow, Germans have a vast vocabulary to describe different depths of inebriation. Six representative categories are included here so that you may better explain someone's condition to the authorities.

Looking-deep-into-one's-stein	Zu tief ins Glas gucken	*Tsoo TEEF innz GLAHS gook-ken*
Becoming-the-monkey	Der hat einen Affen	*Dair haht EI-nen AHF-fen*
Touching-the-barmaid-without-the-permission	Der Bardame ohne Erlaubnis in den Hintern Kneifen.	*Dai BAHR-dah-meh OH-neh air-LOWP-niss in dain HEEN-tairn KNEI-fen.*
Springing-the-leaking	Sich in die Hosen machen	*Seekh in dee HOH-zeh MAH-khayn*
Sucking-the-gravel-in-the-parking-lot	Auf dem Parkplatz in den Kies beißen	*Owf daim PAHRK-plahts in dain KEES BEI-sen*
Dead-as-the-old-Elvishoffer	Tot wie der alte Elvishoffer	*Toht vee dair ahl-teh EL-VEES-hoh-fair*

YOUR OKTOBERFEST EMERGENCY

ktoberfest is Munich's annual carnival of intoxication. Good manners require that you consume alcohol as if it were air. Memorize these emergency phrases.

Hey, guys. Are you able to stand up?	Hallo Sie da. Können Sie gerade stehen?	*Hal-loh SEE dah. KUHN-nen zee geh-RAH-deh SHTAY-en?*
Would you help me carry my friend?	Würden Sie mir meinen Freund tragen helfen?	*VYER-den zee meer mei-nen FROYNT TRAH-gen HELL-fen?*
Thanks, but I don't think pork/ pretzels/hazelnut schnapps can help him now.	Danke, aber Schweinefleisch/ Bretzeln/ Haselnußschnapps wird ihm jetzt wohl nicht helfen.	*DAHN-keh, ah-bair SHVEI-neh-fleish/ BRAY-tseln/HAH-zail-nooss-schnahps veert eem yetst vohl NEEKHT HELL-fen.*
I think he's coming to.	Ich glaube, er kommt wieder zu sich.	*EEHK GLOW-beh, air KOHMMT vee - dair tsoo zeekh.*
Hey! It sounds like he's learned to speak German!	Hey! Es hört sich so an, als hätte er Deutsch gelernt!	*Hay! Ess HUHRT seekh zoh AHN, ahls HEH-teh air DOYCH geh-LAIRNT!*

DOWN AND DIRTY IN THE RATSKELLER

Sigmund Freud was one of history's most fearless explorers—he entered the filthy, twisted minds of the Victorian middle class. Their descendants can be found in the local *Ratskeller*, the restaurant lying beneath every *Rathaus* (town hall). Try a little Freudian lip with your waiter or waitress.

I ordered bratwurst but you brought me bloodwurst.	Ich habe Bratwurst bestellt und dennoch haben Sie mir Blutwurst gebracht.	*Eekh HAH-beh BRAHT-voorst be-SHTAYLT oont DEN-nohkh HAH-ben zee meer BLOOT-voorst geh-BRAHKHT.*
Could it be you have fallen in love with me?	Haben Sie sich etwa in mich verliebt?	*HAH-ben zee SEEKH et-vah in meekh vair-LEEPT?*

(continued)

ACCOMMODATION, FOOD AND DRINK

You have an unconscious wish that I eat your sauerkraut.	Sie wünschen im Unterbewußten, daß ich Ihr Sauerkraut esse.	*Zee VEWH-shen im OON-tair-beh-VOOSS-ten, dahss eekh eer ZOW-air-krowt ess-eh.*
Yet that is clearly a fantasy.	Aber das ist offensichtlich eine Phantasie.	*Ah-bair dahs isst OFF-fen-SEEKHT-leekh ei-neh FAHN-tah-ZEE.*
Naturally, I would enjoy a piece of your strudel.	Natürlich hätte ich gerne ein Stück von Ihrem Strudel.	*Nah-TEWR-leekh heh-teh eekh GAIR-neh ein SHTEWK fohn EE-rem SHTROO-dell.*
I suggest you stop in for a lie on my couch.	Ich würde vorschlagen, Sie kommen vorbei und legen sich eine Weile auf meine Couch.	*Eekh vewr-deh FOR-shlah-gen, zee KOHM-men for-BEI oont LAY-gen seekh ei-neh VEI-leh owf MEI-neh KOWCH.*

HOW TO BECOME A GERMAN DISHWASHER

T he many *Neiberlunders* (restaurateurs) who don't accept credit cards will be upset after you consume barrels of food and alcohol and can't pay in cash. The Wicked Traveler negotiates with aplomb, however, even when surrounded by cleaver-wielding waiters.

You don't accept credit cards!?	Sie akzeptieren keine Kreditkarten!?	*Zee ahk-tsep-TEE-ren KEI-neh KRAY-deet-KAR-ten!?*
The bill seems remarkably high for noodles/ potatoes/cabbage/ organ meats.	Diese Rechnung ist ganz schön hoch für Nudeln/ Kartoffeln/Kohl/ Innereien.	*Dee-zeh REKH-noon(g) isst gahnz shern HOHKH fewr NOO-deln/Kahr TOFF-eln/KOHL/ EEN-nair-EI-en.*
Hmm. I haven't enough Euros to pay the bill.	Hmm. Ich habe nicht genug Euro, um die Rechnung zu bezahlen.	*Hmm. Eekh hah-beh neekht ge-nookh YOU-roh, oom dee RAYKH-noong tsoo bay-TSAH-len.*
I do have some dollar-denominated traveler's checks.	Ich habe einige Dollar-Reiseschecks.	*Eekh hah-beh ei-nee-geh DOH-lahr-REI-zeh-shecks.*

(continued)

ACCOMMODATION, FOOD AND DRINK

Watch it, fella. You're talking about my national currency.	Vorsicht, mein Freund. Sie reden über meine Landeswährung.	*FOR-seekht, mein FROYNT. Zee RAY-den ew-bair mei-neh LAHN-dess-VAIR-oon(g).*
You can check today's newspaper for the exchange rate.	Sie können den Wechselkurs in der heutigen Zeitung nachsehen.	*Zee kuhn-nen dain VECK-sel-koors in dair HOY-tee-gen TSEI-toon(g) NAHKH-zay-en.*
Or I'll return the meal to you.	Oder Sie kriegen das Essen zurück.	*OH-dair zee KREE-gen dahs ESS-en tsoo-REWK.*
With my compliments to the chef.	Mit meinen Komplimenten an den Koch.	*Mit MEI-nen kohm-plee-MEN-ten ahn dain KOHK.*

THE COST OF MONEY

German banks are surrounded by some of the world's thickest bureaucracy. There are almost certainly some good reasons for this. Efforts to get around it will only make matters worse.

I'd like to cash this traveler's check.	Ich möchte diesen Reisescheck eintauschen.	*Eekh MUHKH-teh DEE-zen REI-zeh-sheck EIN-tow-shen.*
My credit cards, passport, driver's license, and a signed photograph of Karl Malden?	Meine Kreditkarten, mein Paß, mein Führerschein und ein Foto mit dem Autogramm von Karl Malden?	*Mei-neh KRAY-dit-KAHR-ten, mein PAHSS, mein FEWR-rair-shein oont ein FOH-toh mit daim OW-toh-GRAHM fohn KAHRL MALL-den?*
No trouble—I have them right here.	Kein Problem— ich habe das alles hier.	*Kein proh-BLAIM-eekh hah-beh dahs ahl-less HEER.*
Would you also like to see my birthmark?	Möchten Sie mein Muttermal sehen?	*MUHKH-ten zee mein MOOT-tair-mahl Zay-en?*
It looks exactly like Munch's *The Scream.*	Er sieht genau wie Munchs *Der Schrei* aus.	*Air zeet gen-NOW vee MUHNKHS dair SCHREI ows.*

ABSOLUTE WURSTS

A trip to the *Metzger* (butcher) can be confusing; the ever-inventive Germans eat more than a thousand varieties of sausage. A few simple questions can help you identify things you wouldn't want to put in your mouth.

Which animal was this?	Was für ein Tier war das?	*VAHS fewr ein TEER vahr dahs?*
Which part?	Welcher Teil?	*Vell-khair TEIL?*
Please just point to the place on your own body.	Bitte zeigen Sie mir die Stelle an Ihrem Körper.	*BIT-teh TSEI-gen zee meer dee SHTEL-leh ahn EER-em KER-per.*
Hmm. That doesn't look very tasty/healthful.	Hmm. Das sieht mir nicht besonders schmackhaft/gesund aus.	*Hmm. Dahs zeet meer NEEKHT beh-zohn-dairz SHMAHK-hahft/ geh-ZUNT ows.*
Did I mention that I've decided to become a vegetarian?	Habe ich erwähnt, daß ich mich entschlossen habe, Vegetarier zu werden?	*Hah-be eekh air-VAINT, dahss eekh meekh ent-SHLOHS-sen hah-beh, VEH-geh-tair-EER tsoo VAIR-den?*

THE WORST OF THE WURSTS

This guide is provided for those who want to identify menu items and avoid trying anything new.

CHARMING GERMAN NAME	ACTUAL STUFFING
Aalgeleewurst*	jellied eels
Cervelatwurst*	scent organs
Gänseleberwurst*	swollen goose livers
Geflügelwurst*	things with wings
Lammzungenwurst*	tongues of lambs
Leberkäswurst*	clotted liver paste
Münchner Weisswurst*	brains of calves
Milzwurst*	slippery spleen meats
Rauhwurst*	assorted sardine parts
Schweineherzwurst*	well-marbled pig hearts
Wurstwurst*	defective wurst

* Indicates Non-Kosher

PHONE CALL FOR MR. KAFKA

I n formerly Communist areas, the German phone system still runs largely on Stalinist technology and attitudes. Operators continue to respond better to orders than to requests.

Operator, what is the area code for Munich?	Was ist die Vorwahl für München?	*VAHS isst dee FOR-vahl fewr MEWN-khen?*
Ha! It is nonsense to say that area codes are classified.	So ein Quatsch zu sagen, daß Vorwahlnummern Geheimsache sind.	*ZOH ein KVAHTCH tsoo ZAH-gen, dahss FOR-vahl-NOOM-mairn geh-HEIM-sah-khe zint.*
Don't you know who I am?	Sie wissen wohl nicht, wer ich bin?	*Zee VISS-en vohl neekht, VAIR eekh bin?*
I happen to have your file right here.	Ich habe zufällig Ihre Akte gerade hier.	*Eekh hah-beh TSOO-fay-leekh EE-reh AHK-teh geh-RAH-deh heer.*
I'll have your hazelnuts in a vise, my friend.	Ich werde Ihre Brötchen unter Beschuß nehmen, meine Gute.	*Eekh VAIR-deh EE-reh BREWT-khen oon-tair beh-SHOOSS NAY-men, mei-neh GOO-teh.*

You'll wish you'd been born in Bulgaria.	Sie werden sich wünschen, in Bulgarien geboren worden zu sein.	*Zee VAIR-den seekh VEWN-shen, in bool-GAHR-ee-en geh-BOH-ren vohr-den tsoo zein.*
Put me through to Munich immediately!	Verbinden Sie mich auf der Stelle mit München!	*Fair-BIN-den zee meekh OWF dair SHTEL-leh mit MEWN-khen!*

POST COMMUNIST

Formerly East German postal workers haven't broken the habit of reading other people's mail. To keep your correspondence private, use the following.

CODE WORD (ENGLISH)	ACTUAL MEANING	CODE WORD (GERMAN)
Gretel	having	*Gretl*
feels	a	*fühlt sich*
quite	good	*ziemlich*
ill	time	*krank*
and	wish	*und*
smells	you	*riecht*
worse	were	*schlimmer*
daily	here	*von einem Tag zum anderen*

SHOPPING FOR LAUGHS

I f money and style mean nothing to you, you might enjoy shopping for clothes in Germany. Berlin has an especially bizarre variety of stores and fashions. Even if you can't afford to buy anything, you can have fun with sales help.

Hey! I've never seen a comedy clothing store before!	Hallo! Ich habe nie zuvor einen Kleiderladen für Komödianten gesehen!	*Hahl-loh! Eekh HAH-beh NEE tsoo-for ein-en KLEI-dair-LAH-den fewr koh-muh-dee-AHN-ten ge-ZAY-en!*
These lederhosen/ jackets/ties are hilarious!	Diese Hosen/ Jacketts/ Krawatten sind einfach umwerfend!	*Dee-zeh HOH-zen/ Jahk-KETS/Krah-VAHT-ten zint ein-fahkh OOM-vair-fent!*
Do you have anything out of the brown area of the spectrum?	Haben Sie etwas außerhalb des braunen Farbspektrums?	*Hah-bayn zee ET-vahs OW-zair-hahlp dess BROW-nen FAHRP-shpeck-troomz?*
What great loden coats/Tyrolean hats/mod shoes!	Was für tolle Lodenmäntel Tirolerhüte/ modische Schuhe!	*Vahs fyoor TOHL-leh LOH-den-MEN-tell/tee-ROH-lair-hew-teh/moh-dish-eh SHOO-eh!*

So heavy/goofy/ German!	So schwer/ vertrottelt/ deutsch!	*Zoh SHVAIR fair-TROHT-tellt DOYCH!*
I'll take them all!	Ich nehme das alles!	*Eekh NAY-meh dahs AHL-less!*
Charge my Barnum & Bailey account.	Stellen Sie es meinem Konto bei Barnum & Bailey in Rechnung.	*SHTEL-len zee ess MEI-nem KOHN-toh bei Barnum & Bailey in REKH-noon(g).*

YOU AND THE SWISS ARMY KNIFE

When shopping for souvenirs, resist salespeople's attempts to sell you a model with more bells and whistles than you really need. German products are expensive enough already.

Hello, I'd like to buy a camera/pair of binoculars/fondue set.	Hallo, ich hätte gerne eine Kamera/Ferngläser/Fonduegeschirr.	*HAHL-loh, eekh heht-teh gair-neh ei-neh KAH-meh-rah/FAIRN-glay-zer/fohn-DEW-geh-SHEER.*
Do you have one without a belt punch/electronic brain?	Haben Sie ein Gerät ohne Lochzange/Elektrogehirn?	*Hah-ben Zee ein geh-RAIT OH-neh LOHKH-tsahng-eh/ay-LEKH-troh-geh-heern?*
It is superior, I'm sure.	Ich bin sicher, es ist von auserlesener Qualität	*Eekh bin SEEKH-er, ess ist fohn OWZ-air-LAY-zen-er kvah-lee-TAIT.*
But I don't need 400 horsepower.	Aber ich brauche keine 400 PS.	*AH-bair eekh BROW-kheh kei-neh FEER-hoon-dairt PS.*
I think I'll just take this commemorative key chain.	Ich denke, ich nehme nur diesen Schlüsselbund als Andenken	*Eekh DINK-eh, eekh NAY-meh NOOR DEE-zen SHLUHS-sell-boont ahls AHN-dink-en.*

SURVIVING THE AUTOBAHN

No trip to Germany would be complete without the testosterone charge of competitive driving in a borrowed car. With enough browbeating, most rental agents will supply you with a car that burns rubber in every gear. Don't settle for less.

I requested an automobile, not a golf cart.	Ich habe ein Auto bestellt und nicht ein Golfmobil.	*Eekh HAH-beh ein OW-toh beh-SHTELLT oont neekht ein GOHLF-moh-beel.*
This child's toy struggles to reach 225 kilometers.	Dieses Kinderspielzeug quält sich ab, 225 Kilometer zu erreichen.	*Dee-zess KIN-dair shpeel-tsoyk KVAILT seekh AHP, TSVEI-hoon-dairt-FUHNF-oont-TSVAHN-tseekh KEE-loh-may-ter tsoo air-REI-khen.*
I refuse to be humiliated by you or by other drivers.	Ich weigere mich, von Ihnen oder anderen Fahrern beleidigt zu werden.	*Eekh VEI-gair-eh meekh, fohn EE-nen oh-dair AHN-dair-en FAHR-airn beh-LEI-dikt tsoo VAIR-den.*
Give me twelve cylinders or a full refund.	Geben Sie mir zwölf Zylinder oder mein Geld zurück.	*GAY-ben zee meer ZVUHLF TSEE-len-dair oh-der mein GELT tsoo-RUHK.*

ROAD CURSES AND FINES

Although you may be fined in Germany for cursing other drivers, it can be richly satisfying. Use this price list to decide what you can afford.

SLUR	TRANSLATION	FINE
Damischer Bulle *DAH-mee-shair-BOOL-leh*	stupid bull	$2,760
Raubritter *ROWB-reet-tair*	robber baron	$2,080
Depp *Depp*	idiot	$1,175
Stinkstiefel *SHTINK-shtee-fell*	smelly boot	$729
Knolle *KNOHL-leh*	tuber	$425
Rchtlfrtzlkraut	(unintelligible)	$100
Wichtigtuer *VEEKH-teekh-too-air*	poo-poo head	2 for 99¢

ROAD SIGNS

Before getting behind the wheel in Germany, be sure to memorize the country's unique road signs.

NO SENSE OF HUMOR
NEXT 1200 KM

BEER HALL AREA
PREPARE STEINS

STRAIGHTAWAY
STOMP DAS PEDAL TO DER METAL

WATCH FOR
FALLING DOLLAR

SLOW:
ELF CROSSING

THE POLICEMAN'S BEAT

Polizei (police officers) are officious and notoriously unhelpful to foreigners. Luckily, they can be paralyzed by anyone who dares to defy them.

Officer, please direct me to Wartburg?	Wachtmeister, können Sie mir sagen, wie ich zur Wartburg komme?	*VAHKHT-mei-stair, KUHN-nen zee meer ZAH-gen, vee EEKH tsoor VAHRT-boorg kohm-meh?*
You want to see my passport?	Sie wollen meinen Paß sehen?	*Zee VOHL-len mei-nen PAHSS ZAY-en?*
Don't be an idiot.	Seien Sie kein Idiot.	*ZEI-en zee KEIN ee-dee-OHT.*
I've got a castle tour in 15 minutes.	Ich habe in 15 Minuten eine Führung durch die Burg.	*Eekh HAH-beh in FUHNF-tsain mee-NOO-ten ei-neh FEW-roon(g) doorkh dee BOORG.*
Maybe you didn't hear me the first time, brick wit.	Vielleicht haben Sie mich beim erstenmal nicht gehört, Sie Hohlkopf.	*Feel-LEIKHT hah-ben zee meekh beim AIR-sten-mahl neekht geh-HUHRT, zee HOHL-kopf.*

Tell me where to find the castle or kiss my dirndl, dachshund breath.	Sagen Sie mir, wo ich die Burg finde, oder küssen Sie mein Dirndl, Sie räudiger Dackel.	*ZAH-gen zee MEER, VOH eekh die BOORG FIN-deh, oh-dair KUHS-sen zee mein DEERN-del, zee ROY-dih-gair DAHK-kel*
Thank you for letting me ride in your squad car.	Danke, daß Sie mich in Ihrem Streifenwagen mitnehmen.	*DAHN-keh, dahss zee meekh in EE-rem SHTREI-fen-VAH-gen MIT-nay-men.*
Now I am sure to reach the castle on time.	Nun bin ich sicher, daß ich die Burg rechtzeitig erreichen werde.	*Noon bin eekh SIKH-er, dahss eekh dee BOORG REKHT-tsei-tikh air-REI-khen vair-deh.*

SERVE AND PROTECT

G erman highway patrol officers are always on the lookout for weak, hesitant drivers who throw kinks into the blur of *Autobahn* traffic. Speak their language and avoid misunderstandings.

What seems to be the problem, officer?	Was scheint das Problem zu sein, Herr Wachtmeister?	*Vahs sheint dahs proh-BLAIM tsoo zein, hair VAHKHT-mei-stair?*
I had to ram him/her off the road, of course.	Ich mußte ihn/sie natürlich von der Straße rammen.	*Eekh MOOSS-teh een/zee nah-TEWR-leekh fohn dair SHTRAH-seh RAHM-men.*
He/she was driving dangerously slow in the fast lane.	Er/Sie fuhr wirklich gefährlich langsam in der Überholspur.	*AIR/ZEE foohr veerk-leekh gey-FAIR-leekh LAHN(G)-zahm in dair EW-bair-HOHL-shpoor.*
No more than 240 kilometers an hour!	Nicht mehr als 240 Stundenkilometer!	*NEEKHT mair ahls TSVAL-hoon-dairt-VEER-tseekh SHTOON-den-kee-loh-may-tir!*

No, thank *you*, officer.	Nein, vielen Dank, Herr Wachtmeister.	*NINE, FEE-len DAHNK, hair VAHKHT-mei-stair*
Keep up the good work!	Machen Sie nur so weiter!	*MAH-khen zee NOOR zoh VEI-tair!*

SOCIALISM THROUGH AUTOMOBILES

The achievements of socialism included dough-like complexions, air pollution you could eat with a spoon, and the Trabant. Compare this car-like object to the pinnacle of West German automotive efforts.

	PORSCHE 911 GT2	TRABANT IRON CHIPMUNK
Ceramic Composite Brakes	✓	
Genuine Pine Gearbox		✓
Fuel Injection	✓	
Coal Chute		✓
Twin-Turbo Flat Six	✓	
Duct Tape		✓
475 Horsepower	✓	
Handy Pull-Starter		✓
Alloy Wheels	✓	
Hamster Wheel		✓

CONFESSIONS OF A SINNER

ermans love to follow rules, and they want you to follow them, too. Jaywalking, for example, is likely to get you a stern lecture from a concerned citizen. Your counterattack should be merciless.

Ha! That was nothing.	Ha! Das war nichts.	*Hah! DAHS vahr NEEKHTS.*
Tuesday I threw a gum wrapper in the town square.	Am Dienstag warf ich ein Kaugummipapier auf den Marktplatz.	*Ahm DEENS-tahk VAHRF eekh ein KOW-goom-mee-pah-PEER owf dain MAHRKT-plahts.*
I unleashed my dog in the park!	Ich habe meine Hundin im Park von der Leine gelassen!	*Eekh HAH-beh mei-neh HUHNT im PAHRK fohn dair LEI-neh geh-LAHS-sen!*
He peed on a bush!	Er hat auf einen Busch gepinkelt!	*Air HAHT owf ei-nen BOOSH geh-PINK-elt!*
Tomorrow I will ride my bicycle on the sidewalk!	Morgen werde ich mein Fahrrad auf dem Bürgersteig fahren!	*MOHR-gen VAIR-deh eekh mein FAHR-rad owf daim BUHR-gair-shteik FAHR-ren!*
Yes! I am a devil/anarchist/American!	Ja! Ich bin ein Teufel/Anarchist/Amerikaner!	*YAH! Eekh bin ein TOY-fel/ah-nar-KHEEST/ah-may-ree-KAH-nair!*

MID-MORNING EXPRESS

I n their rush for seats, some German men inexplicably hurl women and children aside. Freud felt that the seats themselves—made of unvarnished wood in his day—aroused the men sexually. Jung theorized that they regressed to their original ape-like selves and could not stand upright for more than a few moments. Regardless of the diagnosis, these creatures must be reminded of their duties.

Relax, there's no need to insult/ shove/pummel anyone.	Beruhigen Sie sich, sie brauchen keinen zu beleidigen/zu stoßen/mit Fäusten zu schlagen.	*Beh-ROO-ee-gen ZEE zeekh. Zee BROW-khen KEI-nen tsoo beh-LEI-dee-gen/tsoo SHTOH-sen/mit FOY-sten tsoo SHLAH-gen.*
In fact, I would be willing to give you my seat.	Ich bin in der Tat bereit, Ihnen meinen Platz zu überlassen.	*EEKH bin in dair, TAHT beh-REIT, EE-nen MEI-nen PLAHTS tsoo ew-bair-LAHS-sen.*
But your butt is so big you'd need two.	Aber Ihr Hintern ist so groß, daß Sie zwei brauchen.	*AH-bair eer HEEN-tairn ist zoh GROHS, DAHSS zee TSVEI brow-khen.*
You belong in the baggage car.	Sie gehören in den Gepäckwagen	*Zee geh-HUH-ren in dain geh-PECK-vah-gen.*

MYSTERY TRAIN

Train rides across the former frontier between East and West are agonizingly slow because the tracks have different gauges and riders must change trains. Trains in the East also run on a different timetable: the same one you'll find in the Twilight Zone. The conductor will be happy to clear things up for you.

Hello, Madam/ Mister/Comrade Conductor.	Guten Tag, meine Dame/Herr/ Genosse Schaffner.	*Goo-ten TAHK, mei- neh DAH-meh/hair/ geh-NOHS-seh SHAHFF-nair.*
I'm glad to see you're preserving tradition.	Ich freue mich zu sehen, daß Sie die Tradition aufrechterhalten.	*Eekh FROY-eh meekh tsoo ZAY-en, dahss zee dee trah- dee-tsee-OHN OWF-rekht-air- HAHL-ten.*

I haven't seen stone wheels since I was a boy.	Ich habe keine Steinräder gesehen, seit ich ein Junge war.	*Eekh HAH-beh kei-neh SHTEIN-rai-dair geh-ZAY-en, zeit eekh ein YOON(G)-eh vahr.*
But I am confused.	Aber ich bin verwirrt.	*Ah-bair EEKH bin fair-VEERT*
Why are we stopped on this siding?	Warum halten wir an diesem Rangiergleis an?	*Vah-ROOM HAHL-ten veer ahn DEE-zem RAN-geer-gleiss ahn?*
I am growing thirsty/hungry/senile.	Ich werde durstig/hungrig/senil.	*Eekh VAIR-deh DOOR-shtikh/HOON(G)-reekh/zay-NEEL.*
Will we reach Berlin in this decade?	Werden wir Berlin in diesem Jahrtausend erreichen?	*VAIR-den veer Bair-leen in DEE-zem yahr-TOW-zent air-REI-khen?*

THE SPIRIT OF THE RED BARON

E fficient air travel depends on human organization and well-maintained machinery. Germans have extraordinary talents in these two areas, but perfection has yet to be achieved on Lufthansa, the German airline. Feel free to point out glitches to airline employees.

Steward(ess), according to my chronograph, we took off three minutes late.	Steward(ess)! Nach meiner Uhr sind wir mit mehr als drei Minuten Verspätung abgeflogen.	*Steward(ess)! Nakh MEI-nair OOR zint veer mit MAIR ahls DREI mee-NOO-ten fair-SHPAY-toon(g) AHP-geh-FLOW-gen.*
This is sparkling wine, not Champagne.	Das is Sekt und nicht Champagner.	*Dahs ist ZEKT oont NEEKHT shahm-PAHN-er.*
I'm going to complain to the Red Baron himself.	Ich werde mich beim Roten Baron selbst beschweren.	*Eekh VAIR-deh meekh beim ROH-ten bah-ROHN ZELPST beh-SHVAY-ren.*
What? He's dead?	Was? Der ist tot?	*VAHS? Dair ist TOHT?*
Then who the hell is flying the plane?	Wer zum Teufel fliegt denn dann dieses Flugzeug?	*VAIR tsoom TOY-fell fleekt den dahn DEE-zess FLOOK-tsoykh?*

THE FRONT LINES

G ermans may be famous for their efficiency, but, like their French, Italian and Russian neighbors, they aren't in the habit of lining up. Pretending not to see you, they may try to sidle, waddle, elbow and shove past you. Most will show respect for the first-come-first-served rule, but only when gently reminded.

Yo, Dude.	Ja. Sie.	*YAH. ZEE.*
I was here before you came in.	Ich war vor Ihnen hier.	*Eekh vahr FOHR EE-NEN heer.*
And so were these customers, you swine person.	Und so waren es diese Kunden, Sie Schweinehund.	*Oont ZOH vahr-en DEE-zeh KOON-den, zee SHWEIN-HOONT.*
Don't tell us you're in a hurry to eat!	Sagen Sie uns bloß nicht, Sie sind in Eile und müssen schnell was essen!	*ZAH-gen zee oons BLOHSS neekht, zee zint in EI-leh oont muhs-sen shnell vahs ESS-en!*
Food is the last thing you need.	Essen ist das letzte, was Sie brauchen.	*Ess-en isst dahs LETS-teh, vahs zee BROW-khayn.*
Jog to the back of the line, buddy.	Beweg dich an das Ende der Schlange, Kumpel.	*Beh-VAIG deekh ahn dahs EN-deh dair SHLAHNG-eh, KOOM-pell.*

GRIMM TALES OF THE BLACK FOREST

orests are central to many fables and the Black Forest is the granddaddy of them all. Amuse the locals by referring to fairy-tale adventures.

Say, aren't you a cruel dwarf/wolf in disguise?	Sagen Sie, sind Sie nicht ein grausamer Zwerg/ verkleideter Wolf?	*ZAH-gen zee, zint zee neekht ein GROW-zah-mair TSVAIRK/ fair-KLEI-deh-ter VOHLF?*
We seek a golden ring/your head on a platter/a couple of cold beers.	Wir suchen einen goldenen Ring/Ihren Kopf auf einer Platte/zwei Glas kalten Bieres.	*Veer ZOO-khen ei-nen GOLD-en-en RING/ee-ren KOHPF owf ei-nair PLAHT-teh/tsvei glahs kahl-ten BEER-ess.*
What you just said is a riddle to me.	Was Sie gerade sagten, ist mir ein Rätsel.	*Vahs zee geh-RAH-deh zak-ten, ist meer ein RAIT-sell.*
Nevertheless, it sounded mighty rude.	Trotzdem klang es unheimlich rüde.	*TROHTS-daim klahng ess oon-HEIM-leekh REW-deh.*
Be gone, Evil One! Return to your filthy lair!	Gehe dahin, Übler! Zehre zurück in deine dreckige Höhle!	*GAY-eh dah-HIN, EW-blair! KAIR-eh tsoo-REWK in dei-neh DREK-ee-geh HUH-leh!*

IT'S ALL HAPPENING AT THE BERLIN ZOO

On a trip through Berlin, you're almost certain to visit the zoo. A combination transportation hub and menagerie, the zoo attracts many social and biological parasites. Your quick response to their presence will help you avoid infection.

Excuse me. Is this the zoo?	Entschuldigen Sie. Ist das der Zoo?	*Ent-SHOOL-dee-gen zee. Ist DAHS dair TSOH?*
No, I don't need a "date."	Nein, ich brauche keine "Braut."	*NINE, eekh BROW-kheh kei-neh "BROWT."*
Exactly what do you mean when you say "really good time"?	Was meinen Sie genau, wenn Sie sagen: "wirklich gute Zeit"?	*Vahs MEI-nen zee geh-NOW, venn zee ZAH-gen: "VEERK-leekh GOO-teh TSEIT"?*
Fifty euros? That's sickening.	Fünfzig Euro? Da kann einem ja übel werden.	*FUHNF-tseekh You-roh? DAH kahn EI-nem yah EW-bell VAIR-den.*
Who let you out of your cage?	Wer hat dich denn aus dem Käfig herausgelassen?	*VAIR haht deekh denn ows daim KAY-feekh hair-OWS-geh-LAHS-sen?*

CASTLE CRITIQUE

No Bavarian holiday would be complete without a tour of at least one fairy-tale castle. If the owners are home, don't be intimidated by their titles or nobility—impress them with your intelligent questions and comments.

I understand this castle was built many years ago.	Wie ich weiß wurde dieses Schloß vor vielen Jahren gebaut.	*Vee eekh VEISS, voor-deh dee-zess SHLOHSS for FEE-len YAH-ren geh-BOWT.*
Say, that is a handsome bannister.	Das ist aber ein schönes Geländer.	*Dahs ist ah-bair ein SHUH-ness geh-LEN-dair.*
Would you mind if my children took a slide or two?	Hätten Sie was dagegen, wenn meine Kinder einoder zweimal runterrutschten?	*HET-ten zee vahs dah-GAY-gen, venn MEI-neh KIN-dair EIN-oh-dair TSVEI-mahl ROON-tair-ROOCH-ten?*
So, how does Mrs. Ludwig keep up with the dusting?	So, wie kommt Frau Ludwig mit dem Staubwischen nach?	*ZOH, VEE kohmmt frow LOOD-weekh mit daim SHTOWB-vee-shen NAHKH?*

CRIB SHEET TO MAJOR MYTHS

Teutonic myths allow insight into the German character and the plots of endless, impenetrable operas, poems, novels and delusions. These "crib notes" will help you avoid the agony of studying the myths in their original forms.

THE NIBELUNGENLIED, A.K.A. THE RING

Herr Doktor Siegfried wields a sword made by Swiss elves. Herr Doktor Hagen kills him anyway and chucks the Rheingold, an absolutely corrupting treasure, into the Rhine. Most of the fish are killed.

HERR DOKTOR GEORG JOHANN FAUST

In *Faust: The Early Years*, the old doktor sells his soul to Mephistopheles for knowledge, eternal life, a young woman named Gretchen and a Biedermeier dinette set. Faust forgets to ask for Gretchen's immortality or medical insurance. Tragedy ensues.

THE SORROWS OF YOUNG WERTHER

Herr Doktoral Kandidate Werther, a brilliant but dreamy fellow, falls in love with Lotte, a girl with a slow wit and unusually large *Entchen*. He immediately loses her phone number and then can't remember her name. Distraught, he blows his brains out.

THE BADENEST BATHS IN GERMANY

Germany's mineral springs have been popular with rich rheumatic people since the Romans ruled. If you are rich and rheumatic—or just want to feel that way—be sure to visit a spa to get bathed, steamed and pummeled.

Don't allow a host or hostess to order you around. As a paying customer, you can say no to any part of the program.

I don't mind being stark naked in front of a group of stark naked strangers.	Es macht mir nichts aus, vor einer Gruppe völlig nackter Fremder völlig nackt zu sein.	*Ess MAHKHT meer NEEKHTS ows, fohr ei-nair GROOP-peh fuhl-leekh NAHK-tair FREM-dair fuhl-leekh NAHKT tsoo zein.*
As long as they are older and uglier than I.	Solange sie älter und häßlicher sind als ich.	*Zoh-LAHN(G)-eh zee ELL-tair oont HESS-lee-khair zint ahls EEKH.*
Will people be offended if I avert my eyes?	Werden die Leute sich beleidigt fühlen, wenn ich meine Augen abwende?	*VAIR-den dee LOY-teh zeekh beh-LEI-deekht FUH-len, venn eekh MEI-neh OW-gen AHP-venn-deh?*

I will not allow that mud to touch my body.	Ich werde nicht erlauben, das Schlamm meinen Körper zu berühren	*Eekh vair-deh neekht air-LOW-ben, das SHLAHM meinen KUHR-per tsoo beh-RUH-ren.*
I don't care about the curative powers—it's disgusting.	Seine heilenden Kräfte sind mir wurscht; er ist ekelerregend.	*ZEI-neh HEI-len-den KREHF-teh zint meer VOORSHT; air ist AY-kell-RAY-gent.*
By the way, how ill are the other bathers?	Übrigens, wie krank sind die anderen Badenden?	*EW-bree-genz, vee KRAHNK zint dee AHN-dair-en BAH-den-den?*
Can you tell me which ones are contagious?	Können Sie mir sagen, wer von Ihnen ansteckende Krankheiten hat?	*KUHN-nen zee meer ZAH-gen, VAIR fohn ee-nen AHN-shtek-ken-deh KRAHNK-hei-ten HAHT?*

THE PRETTY GOOD OUTDOORS

Germans love the wilderness and have been improving it since about 4000 B.C. They love to hike and climb in the mountains and will be glad to share them with you, especially if you consider every hike a competition—and lose. Nothing upsets them more than criticism of their landscape, no matter how denuded it has become due to industrial development and acid rain. Comment only on the good things about the forest.

Your rugged mountains take my breath away.	Ihre zerklüfteten Berge sind atemberaubend.	*EE-reh tsair-KLUHF-teh-ten BAIR-geh zint AH-tem-beh-ROW-bent.*
Or perhaps it is the lack of oxygen.	Oder vielleicht ist es der Mangel an Sauerstoff.	*Oh-dair feel-LEIKHT ist ess dair MAHN-gell ahn ZOW-air-shtohff.*
I sighted several trees this morning.	Heute morgen erspähte ich mehrere Bäume.	*HOY-teh MOHR-gen air-SHPAY-teh eekh MAIR-eh-reh BOY-meh.*
Also a squirrel!	Auch ein Eichhörnchen!	*OWKH ein EIKH-huhrn-khen!*

I'm glad you've installed gravel paths, handrails, garbage cans, benches and signposts every 100 meters.	Ich bin so froh, daß Sie für all die Kieswege, Geländer, Abfalleimer, Bänke und alle 100 Meter Wegweiser gesorgt haben.	*Eekh bin zoh FROH, dahss zee fewr AHLL dee KEES-vay-geh, Geh-LEN-dair, AHP-fahll-EI-mair, BAIN-keh oont AHL-leh HOON-dairt MAY-tair VAIG-vei-zair geh-ZORKT hah-ben.*
Nevertheless, we are lost.	Trotzdem haben wir uns verlaufen.	*TROHTS-daim hah-ben veer oons fair-LOW-fen.*
Could you direct us to the parking lot?	Könnten Sie uns den Weg zum Parkplatz zeigen?	*KUHN-ten zee OONS dain VAIG tsoom PAHRK-plahts TSEI-gen?*

HOW TO PICK UP A RHEIN MAIDEN

Skiing single is a superb way for guys to meet tanned, limber German women. Once a *Meinhoffer* (dude) is on a chairlift with one, she is immobilized and subject to his clever repartee.

I saw you on the slope.	Ich sah Sie auf der Piste.	*Eekh ZAH zee owf dair PEE-steh.*
What beautiful form you have!	Was für eine tolle Form Sie haben!	*VAHS fewr ei-neh TOHL-leh FOHRM zee HAH-ben!*
Your skiing is good, too.	Sie laufen auch gut Schi.	*Zee LOW-fen owkh goot SHEE.*
Do you like my skis?	Gefallen Ihnen meine Schier?	*Geh-FAHL-len EE-nen mei-neh SHEE-air?*
They are long, yes?	Sie sind lang, nicht wahr?	*Zee zint LAHNG, neekht VAHR?*
Are you aware that ski length corresponds to strength and courage?	Wußten Sie, daß Schilänge mit Kraft und Mut einhergeht?	*VOOSS-ten zee, DAHSS SHEE-lehng-eh mit KRAHFT oont MOOT EIN-hair-GAIT?*
Say, do you like fondue/massage?	Sagen Sie, mögen Sie Fondue/eine Massage?	*ZAH-gen zee, MUH-gen zee fohn-DEW/ei-neh mah-SAH-sheh?*

MAN OR SUPERMAN

Many women like the blond hair, athletic build and haughty demeanor of German men. Crack their arrogance with a few carefully chosen phrases.

Excuse me, do you know a strong/ experienced man who could help me?	Entschuldigen Sie, kennen Sie einen starken/erfahrenen Mann, der mir helfen könnte?	*Ent-SHOOL-dee-gen zee, KEN-nen zee ei-nen SHTAR-ken/air-FAH-ren-en MAHN, dair meer HELL-fen KUHN-teh?*
I'm having trouble with my car.	Ich habe Probleme mit meinem Wagen.	*Eekh HAH-beh proh-BLAY-meh mit MEI-nem VAH-gen.*
Perhaps I need a fresh set of plugs.	Vielleicht brauche ich neue Zündkerzen.	*Feel-LEIKHT BROW-kheh eekh NOY-eh TSUHNT-kair-tsen.*
Whom could I trust to handle a job like that?	Wem könnte ich diesen Job anvertrauen?	*VAIM kuhn-teh eekh dee-zen JOHB AHN-fair-TROW-en?*
When shall I swing by?	Wann soll ich vorbeikommen?	*VAHN ZOLL eekh fohr-BEI-kohm-men?*

ANARCHY RULES

Discos are great places to meet anarchists, artists, and vegetarians. Fashion is an important part of making friends with these people, so be sure to wear the right clothing and admire that of your quarry.

I love your black boots/pants/shirt/jacket/hat/lipstick.	Ich finde Deine Stiefel/Deine Hose/Dein Hemd/Deine Jacke/Deinen Hut/Deinen Lippenstift einfach toll. Alles in Schwarz.	*Eekh FIN-deh dei-neh SHTEE-fell/dei-neh HOH-zeh/dein HEMT/dei-neh YAHK-keh/dei-nen HOOT/dei-nen LEEP-pen-SHTEEFT EIN-fahkh TOHLL. AHL-less in SHVARTS.*
Do you also like my black boots/pants/shirt/jacket/hat/lipstick?	Finden Sie meine schwarzen Stiefel/meine Hose/mein Hemd/meine Jacke/meinen Hut/meinen Lippenstift auch gut?	*Fin-den zee MEI-neh SHVAHR-tsen SHTEE-fell/HOH-zeh/HEMT/YAHK-keh/HOOT/LEEP-pen-SHTEEFT OWKH goot?*
I could see right away you're an alternative person.	Ich habe gleich bemerkt—du bist ain Alternativer.	*Eekh HAH-beh GLEIKH beh-MAIRKT—doo bist ein ahl-TAIR-nah-TEE-fair.*

ENTERTAINMENT & NIGHTLIFE

No one could wear more black than you do.	Keiner könnte mehr Schwarz tragen also du.	*KEI-nair KUHN-teh mair SHVAHRTS trah-gen ahls DOO.*
Let me pay with money from my black wallet and we'll leave on my black bicycle.	Laß mich mit Geld aus meinem schwarzen Portemonnaie zahlen, und wir nehmen dann mein schwarzes Fahrrad.	*LAHSS meekh mit GELT ows mei-nem SHVAR-tsen POHRT-moh-nay TSAH-len, oont veer NAY-men dahn mein SHVAR-tses FAHR-raht.*
What? You're holding out for a black Mercedes?	Was? Du bestehst auf einem schwarzen Mercedes?	*VAHS? Doo beh-SHTAYST owf ein-nem SHVAR-tsen mair-SAY-dess?*

THE WORDS OF LOVE AND PASTRY

T hanks to the fact that low-carb diets have yet to catch on in Germany, visitors there will find some of the most delicious cakes and bread anywhere. In fact, Germans feel such a deep passion for pastry that they use the same phrases with their bakers and lovers. Use these examples to get the dessert you want.

What lovely honey cakes/sugar tarts you have.	Sie haben so schönen Honigkuchen/ so schöne Zuckertorte.	*Zee HAH-ben zoh SHUH-nen HOH-neekh-KOO-khen/zoh SHUH-neh TSOOK-air-TOHR-teh.*
I can't sleep at night thinking of your muffin/ marmalade.	Ich kann in der Nacht nicht schlafen, da ich an Ihre Küchlein/ Marmelade denke.	*Eekh KAHN in dair NAHKHT NEEKHT SHLAH-fen, dah eekh ahn EE-reh KUHKH-lein/mahr-meh-LAH-deh DAIN-keh.*
Give me your finest sticky buns/Bavarian cream.	Geben Sie mir Ihre feinsten klebrigsüßen Brötchen/Ihre feinste bayerische Sahne.	*GAY-ben zee meer EE-rah FEIN-sten KLAY-breekh-ZEWS-sen BRUHT-khen/EE-reh FEIN-steh bei-AIR-ree-sheh ZAH-neh.*

ENTERTAINMENT & NIGHTLIFE

I want to bite your bundt cake.	Ist möchte in Ihren Gugelhupf beißen	*Eekh MUHKH-teh in EE-ren GOO-gel-hoopf BEIS-sen.*
You're killing me.	Sie bringen mich um.	*Zee BREEN(G)-en meekh OOM.*
I adore you.	Ich bete Sie an.	*Eekh BAY-teh zee AHN.*
Same time tomorrow?	Morgen zur gleichen Zeit?	*MOHR-gen tsoor GLEI-khen TSEIT?*

MIX & MATCH MUSICAL COMMENTARY

G ermans believe every civilized person should be able to discuss music. When the subject comes up, show how refined you are by choosing one phrase from each of these columns to create a genuine-sounding comment.

SENTIMENT	ARTIST	ADJECTIVE	NOUN
I long for	**Beethoven's**	**sickeningly beautiful**	**bassoon parts.**
Ich sehne mich nach	Beethovens	schrecklich schönen	Fagottparts.
Eekh ZAY-neh meekh nahkh	*BAY-toh-fens*	*Shrek-leekh SHUH-nen*	*fah-GOHT-pahrts*
I could almost touch	**Mozart's**	**velvety**	**adagio.**
Ich könnte fast berühren	Mozarts	samtenes	Adagio.
Eekh KUHN-teh fahst beh-RYOO-ren	*Moht-tsarts*	*zahm-teh-ness*	*Ah-DAH-jee-oh.*

ENTERTAINMENT & NIGHTLIFE

SENTIMENT	ARTIST	ADJECTIVE	NOUN
I admire	**Wagner's**	**enormous**	**Henrietta.**
Ich bewundere	Wagners	enorme	Henrietta.
Eekh beh VOON-deh-reh	*VAHG-nairs*	*ay-NOHR-meh*	*Hen-ree-AY-teh.*
I bathe my psychic wounds in	**Handel's**	**scanty**	**G chords.**
Ich bade meine Wunden in	Händels	knappen	G-Akkorden.
Eekh BAH-deh mei-neh VOON-den in	*HEN-dells*	*KNAHP-pen*	*GAY-ahk-KOHR-den.*
I was moved by	**Schubert's**	**pulsing bronze**	**princess.**
Ich war gerührt von	Schuberts	impulsiver, braunge-brannter	Prinzessin.
Eekh vahr geh-REWRT fohn	*SHOO-bairts*	*EEM-pool-ZEE-vair, BROWN-geh-BRAHN-tair*	*preen-TSES-seen.*

THE GALLANT DUELIST

T he centuries-old tradition of dueling is dying out in German universities, even in Heidelberg. Swordplay is rarely a part of romantic rivalry today, but physical confrontation can still occur. Use these phrases to avoid personal injury.

She means nothing to me.	Sie bedeutet mir nichts	*Zee beh-DOY-tet meer NEEKHTS.*
I regret ever meeting/kissing/ fondling/ marrying her.	Ich bedauere, sie je getroffen/ geküßt/ gestreichelt/ geheiratet zu haben.	*Eekh beh-DOW-air-eh, zee YAY geh-TROHF-fen/ge-KUHST/geh-SHTREI-khelt/ge-HEI-rah-tet tsoo HAH-ben.*
Yes, I would be happy to cut off your nose at dawn.	Ja, ich würde dir gerne in der Dämmerung die Nase abschneiden.	*YAH, eekh VEWR-deh deer GAIR-neh in dair DEM-mair-oon(g) dee NAH-zeh AHB-schnei-den.*
Unfortunately, my plane leaves in 15 minutes.	Leider fliegt mein Flugzeug in 15 Minuten ab.	*LEI-dair fleekt mein FLOOK-tsoykh in FUHNF-tsain mee-NOO-ten AHP.*
She's all yours.	Sie ist ganz die deine.	*Zee ist GAHNTS dee DEI-neh.*

ESCAPE FROM OOMPAH

O ompah is central to German culture.
To avoid spending precious vacation
time listening to it, use a combination of
realistic-sounding excuses and manipulation.

What a pity. I cannot attend.	Schade. Ich kahn nicht dabeisein.	*SHAH-deh. EEKH kahn NEEKHT dah-BEI-zein.*
The sound of an accordion gives me hives/seizures.	Tut mir leid, aber ich kriege Pickel/Anfälle von Akkordeontönen.	*TOOT meer LEIT, ah-bair eekh KREE-geh PEEK-kell/AHN-fell-eh fohn ahk-KOHR-day-ohn-TUH-nen.*
I'll spend the evening alone.	Ich verbringe den Abend allein.	*Eekh fair-BREEN(G)-eh dain AH-bent ah-LEIN.*
There's a documentary tonight about German regional costumes/cheeses!	Und es gibt im fernsehen einen Dokumentarfilm über deutsche Trachten/Käse!	*Oont es GEEPT im FAIRN-zay-en ei-nen DOH-KOO-men-TAHR-feelm ew-bair DOY-cheh TRAHKH-ten/KAY-zeh!*
Could I borrow your Porsche while you're out?	Darf ich deinen Porsche borgen, während du weg bist?	*Dahrf eekh DEI-nen POR-sheh bohr-gen, vair-ent doo VAIK bist?*

SURVIVING GERMAN ROMANTICISM

A visitor who becomes intimate with a lonely *Hausfrau* or traveling salesman may need these phrases to deal with big issues in a sensitive, diplomatic way.

My darling, I've never slept with such a robust person before.	Mein Schatz, ich habe bisher noch nie mit so einem solchen Kraftprotz geschlafen.	*Mein SHAHTS, eekh HAH-beh BEESS-hair nohkh NEE mit ZOH ei-nem KRAHFT-prohts geh-SHLAH-fen.*
I fear you will roll over and crush me like a Moselle grape.	Ich fürchte, du wirst dich umdrehen und mich wie eine Moseltraube zerquetschen.	*Eekh FEWRKH-teh, doo VEERST deekh oom-DRAY-en oont MEEKH vee EI-neh MOH-zell-TROW-bee tsair-KVET-shen.*
Your breath/gas smells like sauerkraut from hell.	Dein Atem/ Gepfurze riecht wie höllisches Sauerkraut.	*Dein AH-tem/geh-PFOOR-tseh reekht vee HUHL-lee-shess ZOW-air-krowt.*
If you don't mind, my pumpkin, I'll sleep on the sofa.	Wenn Du nichts dagegen hast, mein Kürbis, schlafe ich auf dem Sofa.	*Venn doo NEEKHTS dah-GAY-gen hast, mein KER-biss, SHLAH-feh eekh owf daim ZOH-fah.*

MAGIC MOUNTAIN OF EUROS

To do business in Germany you must follow German protocol. That means razor-sharp promptness, complete titles and groveling.

Although almost all the business people you meet will speak English and hold doctorates, they will appreciate your crude attempts to flatter them in their native tongue.

The very honorable mister doctor Klodhopper.	Sehr verehrter Herr Doktor Klodhopper.	*Zair fair-AIR-ter hair OOHK-tohr Klodhopper.*
We need more of those fine products of yours, mister esteemed doktor, sir.	Wir benötigen mehr Ihrer hervorragenden Produkte, werter Herr Doktor.	*Veer beh-NUH-tee-gen MAIR EE-rair hair-fohr-RAH-gen-den proh-DOOK-teh, vair-ter hair DOHK-tohr.*
When our customers see the words "MADE IN GERMANY," they whip out their credit cards without another thought.	Wenn unsere Kunden die Worte "MADE IN GERMANY" sehen, zücken sie ihre Kreditkarten, ohne nachzudenken.	*Venn OON-zair-eh KOON-den dee VOHR-teh "MADE IN GERMANY" ZAY-en, TSUHK-ken zee ee-reh KRAY-deet-KAHR-ten, oh-neh NAHKH-tsoo-dain-ken.*

(continued)

BUSINESS

We are short in the euro department, however.	Wir sind allerdings, was die euro angelangt, knapp bei Kasse.	*VEER zint AHL-lair-din(g)z, vahs dee You-roh AHN-be-lahnkt, KNAHP bei KAHS-seh.*
Would you consider taking an out-of-continent promissory note?	Würden Sie eventuell einen nicht kontinentalen Schuldschein akzeptieren?	*VEWR-den zee ay-ven-too-ELL ei-nen NEEKHT kohn-tee-nen-TAHL-en SHOOLT-shein ahk-tsep-TEE-ren?*

PROMPTNESS HINTS

Politeness requires that you break the plane of the building entrance at the appointed hour; therefore you are expected either to ring the bell or knock four seconds before the agreed appointment time. Other hints are:

• When making a date with anyone, synchronize watches to the nearest 100th of a second.

• When calculating travel time, consider drag coefficients, wind direction and speed, and body fat.

AUTOGESPRÄCHE

A s every red-blooded German businessman loves cars, the subject makes for good business talk. Use these questions to pave the way with your hosts.

Who makes the most intimidating cars: BMW, Mercedes or Porsche?	Wer macht die einschüchternsten Autos: BMW, Mercedes oder Porsche?	*VAIR mahkt dee ein-SHUHKH-tairn-sten OW-tohs? BAY-EM-VAY, mair-KAY-dess oh-dair POHR-sheh?*
Which will be the first to break the sound barrier?	Welches wird als erstes die Schallmauer durchbrechen?	*VEL-khess veerd ahls AIR-stess dee SHAHLL-mow-air DOORKH-brekh-en?*
Are any of them able to clear a path through bumper-to-bumper traffic?	Sind irgendwelche davon in der Lage, sich im Stau klare Bahn zu verschaffen?	*Zint EER-gent vell-kheh da-FOHN in dair LAH-geh, seekh im SHTOW KLAR-eh BAHN zu fair-SHAHF-fen?*
Do you agree that air-to-air missiles should be standard equipment?	Meinen Sie, daß Luft-Luft-Raketen zur Standard-ausrüstung gehören sollten?	*Mei-nen zee, dahss LOOFT-looft-rah-KAY-ten tsoor SHTAHN-dart-OWS-REWS-toon(g) geh-HUH-ren ZOHLL-ten?*

THE INEVITABLE THANK-YOU NOTE

E xperienced travelers write prompt thank-you notes to hosts and hostesses. They are thus invited to return and may avoid troubles like irksome hotel and restaurant bills. It's not a bad idea to remind your benefactors of your value as a friend, as in this typical letter.

Dear Miss/Mrs./Mister/Doktor,	Sehr geehrte Frau/Sehr geehrter Herr Doktor.
Our little drive was thrilling.	Unsere kleine Fahrt war aufregend.
Your car is like a missile.	Ihr Wagen ist wie eine Rakete.
Now I have terrible nightmares.	Nun have ich schreckliche Alpträume.
Don't worry that you were overtaken on the *Autobahn*.	Machen Sie sich nichts daraus, daß Sie auf der Autobahn überholt wurden.
It could happen to anyone.	Das kann jedem passieren.
It will be our secret.	Es bleibt unser Geheimnis.
Thanks again,	Nochmals vielen Dank,

Wicked
ITALIAN

Le perquisizioni sono contrarie alla mia religione.

Strip searches are against my religion.

*Lay pair-KWEEZ-eats-ee-OWN-ay SO-noh cone-TRAR-ee-ay
AH-lah MEE-ah ray-lee-JOAN-ay.*

CONTENTS

FOOD AND DRINK

SHOPPING AND SIGHTSEEING

RELIGION, POLITICS, AND SPORTS

THOSE FRIENDLY ITALIANS

WELCOME TO ITALY

Italians have been perfecting civilization for so long that it looks effortless. What's important in Italy? They've been narrowing it down to the essentials for thousands of years: sunshine, love, silky firm cheeses, romance, roasted garlic, kissing, table wine, passion, a perfectly ripe fig.

You, as a visitor, can fit into the scenery nicely. If you don't yet know the magic of a Roman sunset, someone will be pleased to help you understand it, and throw in the Roman midnight and dawn to boot. If you've never gotten

completely high on coffee, an Italian will gladly get you hooked. If you pay close attention to the rules of restrained behavior, someone will be pleased to help you forget them.

Italians will love you in the same way they love a good prosciutto: they will admire your color and your firm, lightly-marbled flesh. They may compare your aroma to that of a fig. Then they will devour you.

And even before the last morsels of your body and soul have been consumed, they'll be thinking about the next course.

If being torn to pieces and eaten alive sounds like the perfect vacation experience, this book will help you choose exactly whose menu you end up on.

If you prefer instead to see a few museums and do a little shopping, this book will help you stay out of the slaughterhouse altogether.

Wicked Italian is meant to transform you into a complete traveler, capable of subtle understanding, intelligent discourse, and effective verbal assault.

Buona Fortuna.

HAND-TO-HAND CONVERSATION

I n order to have the slightest chance of making yourself understood in Italy, you need to take a little care in pronunciation, and use a few basic hand motions. Gestures clarify the underlying meaning of Italian phrases.

The most popular gesture is made with the fingertips of one hand drawn together, chest high, pointing skyward, while the hand makes little bouncing motions. This gesture adds emphasis to any statement or question, such as *"Ma che sei scemo!"* (You nitwit!) and *"Grazie mille per aver rovesciato il sugo sulla mia cravatta nuova"* (Thank you very much for spilling sauce on my new tie.) Two hands are twice as emphatic as one.

One of the most famous Italian gestures, biting the middle knuckle of the index finger, means either a) *"Ti spezzerei in due"* (I'll break you in half) or b) *"Sei troppo sexy; non lo sopporto"* (You're too sexy; I can't stand it).

Italians have a gesture that replaces the relatively unwieldy British phrase "wink, wink, nudge, nudge." The index finger is placed just below the eye, touching the cheek, pulling the lower eyelid down ever so slightly. *"Ci capiamo, eh?"* (We understand each other, eh?)

The key dinner-table gesture has the index finger pointing into the cheek like a pistol, turning back and forth. The eyes are rolled toward heaven. *"Che cuoca!"* (What a chef!)

Every traveler needs a gesture to express general disdain. In Italy, the lower lip is extended. A flat hand is held horizontally with the palm downward and brushed against the chin as if feeling whiskers. *"Non me ne importa un accidente."* (I don't give a darn.)

LINGUISTIC DISCLAIMER

Because the Italian language is one of complex diction, pronunciation, and gesticulation, no book can prepare readers for every eventuality or even convey foolproof phonetic information to the typical tone-deaf tourist.

Therefore, the author and his publisher, editors, translators, agents, attorneys, bodyguards, and heirs must hereby deny and firmly push away from their persons all responsibility for any intercultural misunderstandings that result in embarrassing errors or gaffes, unintended insults, wild accusations, fisticuffs, general riot, total war, or anchovies.

CLASSIC BORDER PLEAS

The Italian frontier is fairly porous; innocent people entering the country may not even see an *agente di dogana* (customs agent). Visitors who carry *contrabbando*, however, are usually met at the airport by heavily armed soldiers and carnivorous dogs.

I was not at my best when the photo was taken.	Non ero molto in forma quando ho fatto la foto.	*Noan AIR-oh MOLE-toh een FORM-ah KWAN-doh oh FAH-toh lah FOH-toh.*
I have nothing to declare.	Non ho nulla da dichiarare.	*Noan oh NOOL-ah dah DEE-kyah-RAR-ay.*
Well, not much, anyway. Nice doggie!	Beh, non molto. Bel cagnolino!	*Beh, noan MOLE-toh. Bell CON-yoh-LEAN-oh!*
I don't think you want to look in there.	Non credo che lei voglia guardare anche lì dentro.	*Noan CRAY-doh hay lay VOLE-yah gwar-DAR-ay ONK-ay lee DEN-troh.*
I've never seen that before.	Non ho mai visto quella cosa prima d'ora.	*Noan oh my VEEST-oh KWELL-ah COZE-ah PREE-mah DORE-ah.*

Ah ha! This isn't my bag!	Ah ah! Questa non è la mia valigia!	*Ah ah! KWEST-ah noan ay lah MEE-ah vah-LEE-jah!*
Strip searches are against my religion.	Le perquisizioni sono contrarie alla mia religione.	*Lay pair-KWEEZ-eats-ee-OWN-ay SO-noh cone-TRAR-ee-ay AH-lah MEE-ah ray-lee-JOAN-ay.*
What's that rubber glove/ flashlight for?	A cosa serve quel guanto di gomma/ quella pila?	*Ah COZE-ah SAIR-vay kwell GWON-toh dee GOME-ah/kwell-ah pee-lah?*
Wait. I'll confess.	Aspetti. Confesso.	*Ah-SPETT-ee. Cone-FESS-oh.*

ENDING TAXI TERROR

Frequent travelers to Italy are familiar with the symptoms of Taxi Terror: feverish prayer, piercing screams, loose bowels, and cardiac arrest.

But there is hope. Every taxi ride doesn't have to feel like your last. Brace yourself, close your eyes, and repeat these phrases to yourself:

"This driver is a professional."

"This driver is accurate to within millimeters, even at high speeds."

"This driver carries full liability insurance."

If your vehicular hysteria is not soothed by these mantras, or you think you're being cheated on the fare, repeat these phrases to the driver.

Please slow down.	Rallenti, per favore.	*Rah-LENT-ee, pair fah-VORE-ay.*
I'd like to go to the train station, not into orbit.	Vorrei andare alla stazione, non in orbita.	*Vore-AY on-DAR-ay AH-lah STOT-zee-OWN-ay, noan in ORB-eet-ah.*
So this is the new Italian fighter jet.	Quindi, questo è il nuovo aereo da combattimento italiano!	*KWEEN-dee, KWEST-oh ay eel NWOH-voh ah-AIR-ay-oh coam-BAT-ee-MENT-oh ee-tal-YON-oh.*

Ingenious camouflage!	Ingegnosa mimetizzazione!	*Een-jen-YOH-sah mee-may-teet-ZOT-zee-OWN-ay!*
I don't feel well.	Non mi sento bene.	*No mee SENT-oh BAY-nay.*
Would you like to see what I had for lunch?	Vuole vedere cosa ho mangiato a pranzo?	*Voo-OH-lay vay-DARE-ay COH-za oh mahn-JAH-toh ah PRAN-zoh?*
If you don't slow down, I'll barf.	Se non rallenta, vomito.	*Say noan rah-LENT-ah, VOME-eet-oh.*

UNDERSTANDING YOUR FARE

The amount shown on an Italian taxi meter is often well below the price quoted by the driver. His calculation is based upon a formula rumored to be the metered fare multiplied by $p^2 + h/2 + t + (1000s - 10k)/x$, where p represents the number of passengers, h the number of bags, t the number of hours past 8:00 P.M., s the cost of your shoes in euros, k your weight in kilograms, and x anything he damn well pleases. Some negotiation is possible, but most drivers expect to get the fare they state, up to fifty percent beyond what's on the meter.

DOING THE LOCOMOTION

Men who hope to meet Italian women on trains will need more than body language. They'll also need semiplausible opening lines, silky voices, and expensive cologne. Armed with these accoutrements, Englishmen and Americans have a slight advantage over their Italian counterparts. We are thought to be more sincere.

Traditional railroad seduction begins with a long conversation.

Pardon me. Could you recommend any vineyards or restaurants in Tuscany?	Scusi, può indicarmi qualche vigna o ristorante in Toscana?	*SKOO-see, pwoh EEN-dee-CAR-mee KWALL-kay VEEN-yah oh REEST-oh-RONT-ay een toe-SKAH-nah?*
How did Milan surpass Paris as the capital of fashion and cuisine?	Com'è che Milano ha superato Parigi ed è diventata la capitale della moda e della cucina?	*Coh-MAY kay mee-LON-oh ah SOOP-air-OT-oh pah-REE-jee ed ay DEE-ven-TOT-ah lah COP-ee-TAL-ay DELL-ah MODE-ah ay DELL-ah coo-CHEEN-ah?*
Tell me about Garibaldi.	Mi racconti di Garibaldi.	*Mee rah-CONE-tee dee gar-ee-BALD-ee.*

Why are Italian women so naturally graceful?	Perché le donne italiane sono per natura così di classe?	*Pair-KAY lay DON-ay eet-AL-ee-AH-nay SO-no pair nah-TURE-ah coh-SEE dee CLASS-ay?*
How unfaithful are Italian men, really?	Quanto sono infedeli, in realtà, gli uomini italiani?	*KWON-toh SO noh EEN-fee-DAY-lee, een ray-AL-ee-TAH, lyee WHOA-mee-nee ee-tal-YON-ee?*

NOTE TO MEN

Avoid sitting near, speaking to, or looking at the mother, sister, wife, daughter, niece or nanny of any successful Sicilian businessman or of any such businessman's personal friend. Do not even think of such a man's grand-daughter.

TRAIN TRAVEL TIPS

Italians have an optimistic way of describing trains. The *diretto* and *accelerato* are local trains, which stop not only at every station but also between stations.

Each time the train stops, more people get on and start fresh arguments about who has reserved what seat. Therefore, nonstop trains should be taken whenever possible. These are the *espresso* and the *rapido*, the real express trains.

The *bigliettaio* (ticket collector) and *ferroviere* (conductor) will be only too happy to help you enjoy and understand your train ride. For a small tip they might even kick somebody out of your seat.

Once you've settled into your compartment, you may find that trains are a great place to get in touch with Italians, whether you want to or not.

THROWING THE SWITCH

A crowded train compartment isn't nearly as romantic as an empty one. People who want to avoid getting to know their fellow train travelers need a few pointed phrases either to stop conversations in their tracks or derail them completely.

Do you do your own tailoring?	Fa i suoi vestiti da solo?	*Fah ee swoy ves-TEET-ee dah solo?*
And you cut your own hair, too?	E si taglia anche i capelli?	*Ay see TALL-ya ONK-ay ee cah-PELL-ee?*
Have you accepted Jesus Christ as your personal savior?	Lei ha accettato Gesù Cristo come il suo salvatore?	*Lay ah AH-chay-TOT-oh jay-ZOO CREEST-oh COH-may eel SOO-oh SAL-vah-TORE-ay?*
Want to see a really big boil?	Vorrebbe vedere un vero e proprio foruncolone?	*Vore-ABE-ay vay-DARE-ay oon VAIR-oh ay PRO-pree-oh for-OON-coh-LOH-nay?*
Let's discuss your insurance needs.	Parliamo della sua assicurazione.	*Par-lee-YAH-mo DELL-ah SOO-ah ah-seh-coo-rah-zee-OH-nay.*

YOU CAN WIN AT HOTEL NEGOTIATION

An unscrupulous hotel manager may attempt to palm off an inferior room on unsuspecting tourists, or to extract a *mancia* (literally, tip; actually, bribe) in exchange for a room by insisting that the hotel is full.

We made these reservations six months ago.	Abbiamo riservato sei mesi fa.	*Ah-bee-OM-oh REE-zare-VOT-oh SAY MAY-zee fah.*
Then we will sleep here in the lobby.	Allora dormiamo nella lobby.	*Ah-LORE-ah DOR-mee-YOM-oh NELL-ah LOBE-ee.*
We reserved a room with a view.	Avevamo riservato una camera con vista.	*AH-vay-VOM-oh REE-zare-VOT-oh OON-ah COM-air-ah cone VEEST-ah.*
The sheets are still damp.	Le lenzuola sono ancora umide.	*Lay lens-WHOA-la SO-no on-CORE-ah OOM-ee-day.*
What is that smell?	Cos'è quell'odore?	*Coze-AY kwell-oh-DORE-ay?*
Something is living in the bathroom.	C'è qualcosa che si muove nel bagno.	*Chay kwall-COZE-ah kay see moo-OH-vay nell BON-yo.*
There is no hot water.	Non c'è acqua calda.	*Noan chay OCK-wah CALD-ah.*

The cold water is brown.	L'acqua fredda è marrone.	*LOCK-wah FRAID-ah ay mah-RONE-ay.*
Is this a towel or a postage stamp?	È un asciugamano o un francobollo?	*Ay oon ah-SHOOG-ah-MON-oh oh oon FRONK-oh-BOWL-oh?*
Four stars my ass!	Quattro stelle un accidente!	*KWAH-troh STELL-ay oon OTCH-ee-DENT-ay!*
Get me a taxi.	Mi chiami un taxi.	*Me KYAH-mee oon taxi.*
This is a much better room. Thank you.	Questa stanza va molto meglio. Grazie.	*KWEST-ah STON-zah vah MOLE-toh MAIL-yoh. GROT-zee-ay.*
Here's something for your trouble.	Questo è per il disturbo.	*KWEST-oh ay pair eel dee-STAIR-boh.*

AMAZING VENICE

One of the pleasures of Venice is locating your hotel. The city's narrow, crooked streets create nothing less than a maze, albeit an exceptionally charming one. If you don't mind cheating a little, carry a piece of chalk with you and, as you walk away from your hotel in the morning, mark the corners of buildings with small arrows pointing back the way you came. That will give you a fair chance of getting back to your hotel by midnight.

FENDING OFF GYPSY CURSES

Because of its proximity to Eastern Europe, Italy has more than its share of the permanent tourists known as Gypsies. If you don't give a *zingara* (Gypsy woman) money on demand, she will curse your descendants, your rental car, your stockbroker, and your reproductive organs. Then her children will pick your pockets.

They usually work in pairs: One slobbers on you, eyes crossed, while the other rummages through your clothing for valuables and unusual postcards.

The threat of a *schiaffo* (slap) may be enough to disperse the urchins, but keep these phrases on your tongue for emergencies.

I haven't any coins.	Non ho soldi spiccioli.	*Noan oh SOLE-dee SPEECH-oh-li.*
Now get lost.	Allora, vattene.	*Ah-LORE-ah, VAH-tay-nay.*
On your mother's grave!	Sulla tomba di tua madre!	*SOO-lah TOME-bah dee TOO-ah MAH-dray!*
And may your last two teeth rot by Christmas.	Che ti marciscano i denti prima di Natale!	*Kay tee mar-CHEES-kah-noh ee DENT-ee PREE-mah dee nah-TAL-ay!*

Okay, here's fifty cents.	OK, ecco cinquanta centesimi.	*Oh kay, EK-oh cheen-KWAN-tah chayn-TAY-zee-mee*
Now, leave us alone.	Adesso, lasciaci in pace.	*Ah-DAYS-soh, LOSH-ah-chee in PAH-chay.*
Stop thief!	Al ladro!	*Ahl LAH-droh!*
Arrest these children.	Arresti questi bambini.	*Ah-REST-ee KWEST-ee bam-BEAN-ee.*

A ROSE IS A RUSE

Many Gypsies sell single red roses wrapped in plastic. Travelers with foresight will buy one of these mummified blooms on Day One. The rose can be kept indefinitely in a pocket or purse for display when flower sellers appear.

THE ITALIAN PHONE SYSTEM

talian phones are scarce and unreliable. Callers must dial slowly, but not too slowly, spacing the numbers evenly. Long-distance rates are simple: Each thirty-minute call costs as much as first-class airfare to the same location.

Operator? I'd like to call New York.	Centralinista? Vorrei chiamare New York.	*Chentrah-lee-NEEST-ah? Vore-AY kyah-MAR-ay new york.*
Please speak more slowly.	Parli più lentamente, per favore.	*PAR-lee pyu LENT-ah-MENT-ay, pair fah-VORE-ay.*
Could I have an English-speaking operator?	Può passarmi una centralinista che parli inglese?	*Pwoh poss-ARE-me OON-ah chentrah-lee-NEEST-ah kay PAR-lee een-GLAZE-ay?*
Are you speaking English now?	Parla inglese allora?	*PAR-lah een-GLAZE-ay ah-LORE-ah?*
How long will it take to get through?	Quanto ci vorrà per avere la comunicazione?	*KWON-toh chee vore-AH pair ah-VAIR-ay la coh-MOON-ee-COT-zee-OWN-ay?*

I can wait for only four days.	Posso aspettare solo quattro giorni.	*POE-soh ah-spet-TAR-ay solo KWAH-troh JOR-nee.*
How much will that cost?	Quanto verrà a costare?	*KWON-toh vair-AH ah coast-AR-ay?*
Make that a collect call, please.	A spese del ricevente, per favore.	*Ah SPAZE-ay dell reech-ay-VENT-ay, pair fah-VORE-ay.*

PRAYER TO SAINT ILARIA, VIRGIN OF NAPLES

Holy Virgin Ilaria, Your Revered Pureness, Only Virgin of Naples, allow me to get his/her phone number, the blonde one by the bar. I swear that my intentions are entirely honorable, Your Stubbornness. Amen.

Santa Ilaria Vergine, Sua Venerata Purezza, Unica Vergine di Napoli, aiutami ad avere il numero di telefono del biondo/della bionda del bar. Giuro che le mie intenzioni sono più che serie, Sua Ostinazione. Amen.

ITALIAN DRUGS YOU MAY NEED

Drugs are the only answer to some travel disasters. In order to get the right *medicina* (drug), one must know brand names and their pronunciations.

DISASTER	DRUG OF CHOICE	NOTE
Headache	*Novalgina (NO-vall-JEEN-ah)*	*Liquid analgesic; not supposed to upset stomach.*
Overeating	*Diger Seltz (DEE-jair seltz)*	*Might as well buy the twelve-pack.*
Sleeplessness	*Mogadon (MOAG-ah-DOAN)*	*Probably not strong enough to overcome Italian espresso.*
Constipation	*Guttalax (GOOT-ah-LOX)*	*The amount of olive oil in the Italian diet should render this drug unnecessary.*

HOW AND WHEN TO QUOTE DANTE

Dante Alighieri was not your average Florentine poet. He was and is Italy's Shakespeare.

Natives will be flattered by non-Italian visitors who quote Dante. But quoting *il poeta della Divina Commedia* (the poet of the *Divine Comedy*) at length is considered pompous. Better to drop a few lines in appropriate situations.

AT THE STATION ENTRANCE DURING A GENERAL STRIKE:

Abandon all hope, ye who enter here.	Lasciate ogni speranza, voi che entrate.	*Losh-AH-tay OWN-yee spare-ON-za, voy kay en-TROT-ay.*

AFTER A REALLY HUGE HELPING OF PASTA AL PESTO:

There is no greater ache than to remember the happy times in misery.	Non c'è maggior dolore che ricordarsi del tempo felice nella miseria.	*Noan chay mah-JORE doh-LOAR-ay kay RE-core-DAR-see dell TEMP-oh fay-LEECH-ay NELL-ah mee-ZAIR-ee-ah.*

AT A PASSING BUSLOAD OF TOURISTS TACKIER THAN THOU:

O foolish creatures, what ignorance is this which torments you?	O creature sciocche, quanta ignoranza è quella che v'offende?	*Oh crayah-TURE-ay SHOKE-ay, KWON-tah EEN-yore-ONZ-ah ay KWELL-ah kay voh-FEND-ay?*

ELEMENTARY CURSING

I talian is a sharp, crisp language, and Mediterranean tempers are hot. As a result, Italians enjoy a special expertise in cursing.

Hurting someone's feelings is plenty of fun until he breaks your legs. As with all curses, these are best used when the subject is well out of earshot.

Turd.	Stronzo.	*STRONE-zo.*
Cretin.	Cretino.	*Cray-TEEN-oh.*
Wimp (human larva).	Larva umana.	*LAR-vah oo-MON-ah.*
He is a worm.	Lui è un verme.	*LOO-ee ay oon VAIR-may.*
She's brainless.	Lei è senza cervello.	*Lay ay SEN-sah chair-VELL-oh.*
They are all bad eggs.	Son tutte uova marce.	*Soan TOOT-ay WHOA-vah MAR-chay.*
Screw yourself.	Vaffanculo.	*VA-fon-COOL-oh.*
You have no class (literally, "You're a dockworker.")	Lei è uno scaricatore di porto.	*LAY ay OON-oh SCAR-ee-cah-TORE-ay dee PORT-oh.*

An utter scoundrel, and ugly, too.	Un perfetto mascalzone, e anche brutto.	*Oon-pair-FETT-oh MAH-scal-ZONE-ay, ay ONK-ay BRUTE-oh.*
Complete asshole.	Proprio uno stronzo.	*PRO-pree-oh OON-oh STRONE-zo.*
Filthy parasite.	Sporco parassita.	*SPORE-coh PAR-ah-SEET-ah.*
Hateful fool.	Odioso zuccone.	*OH-dee-OH-soh zoo-CONE-ay.*
Your father is as smart as a chicken.	Tuo padre è un pollo.	*TOO-oh PAH-dray ay oon POLE-oh.*
May your children have the faces of baboons.	Ti possano venire dei figli con la faccia da babbuini.	*Tee POE-son-oh ven-EER-ay day FEEL-yee cone lah FOTCH-ah dah BOB-oo-EEN-ee.*

DRIVE AND SURVIVE

THE AUTOMOBILE: AN ITALIAN LOVE AFFAIR

Because gas is so expensive, few Italians can afford to drive Ferraris, Lamborghinis, or the larger Maseratis. Instead, they endow their Fiats and Alfas with features more common on exotic cars, such as delicate fuel-injection systems and impossible-to-find parts.

Travelers who plan to drive in Italy should learn a little authentic car talk in order to speak to service-station employees and mechanics.

Fill it up, please.	Il pieno, per favore.	*Eel pee-AY-noh, pair fah-VORE-ay.*
Premium. I need that extra horsepower.	Super. Ho bisogno di più potenza.	*SOOP-air. Oh bee-ZONE-yoh dee pyu poh-TENZ-ah.*
Only eighty euros? Hell of a deal.	Soltanto ottanta euro? Che buon affare.	*Sole-TONTO-oh oh-TONT-ah you-roh? Kay bwone ah-FAR-ay.*
Oh my God! What's that sickening sound?	Oh mio Dio! Cos'è quell'orribile rumore?	*Oh MEE-oh DEE-oh! Coze-AY kwell-ore-EEB-ee-lay roo-MORE-ay?*

Perhaps it's the transmission/ engine/exhaust.	Forse è il cambio/ motore/tubo di scappamento.	*FOR-say ay eel COM-bee-oh/moh TORE-ay/TOO-bo dee SCAH-pah-MENT-oh.*
Can it be fixed? How long will it take?	Si può riparare? Quanto ci vorrà?	*See pwoh ree-par-ARE-ay? KWON-toh chee vore-AH?*
Where may we buy train tickets?	Dove possiamo comprare i biglietti del treno?	*DOH-vay POE-see-OM-oh coam-PRAR-ay ee beel-YET-ee dell TRAIN-oh?*

PRAYER TO SAINT LAURA OF ROME

Saint Laura, Princess of Meter Maids, Mother of Tiny Cars, please provide us with a legal parking space in Trastevere this Saturday night. Two hours is all we ask, Your Holy Bureaucracy.

Santa Laura, Principessa delle Vigilesse, Madre delle Piccole Auto, ti preghiamo di aiutarci affinché possiamo trovare un parcheggio a Trastevere questo sabato sera. Due ore è tutto ciò che chiediamo, Sua Santa Borocrazia.

LYING TO POLICEMEN: THE NATIONAL PASTIME

The stupidity of *carabinieri*, the Italian military police, is so legendary that a garden slug would be embarrassed to join their ranks.

No one knows how the military finds replacements for the hundreds of officers who annually shoot themselves with pistols they thought weren't loaded, set their pants on fire, and drive off cliffs in broad daylight. Yet fresh *carabinieri* are found, ready for long hours, low pay and the scorn of a nation. If you should happen to meet one, use some smooth talk to settle any misunderstanding.

Is there a problem, officer?	C'è qualcosa che non va, agente?	*Chay kwall-COZE-ah kay noan vah, ah-JENT-ay?*
I thought the light was green.	Mi sembrava che il semaforo fosse verde.	*Mee sem-BRAH-vah kay eel same-AH-fore-oh FOSSE-ay VAIR-day.*
A one-way street? Is that so!	Senso unico? Davvero!	*SEN-soh OON-ee-coh? Dah-VAIR-oh!*
I am truly sorry.	Mi dispiace davvero.	*Mee DEE-spee-YOTCH-ay dah-VAIR-oh.*

DRIVE AND SURVIVE

Honestly, I wasn't behind the wheel.	Ma a dire il vero, non stavo guidando io.	*Mah ah DEER-ay eel VAIR-oh, noan STAH-voh gwee-DON-doh EE-oh.*
That was my twin brother/sister.	Quello/a era il mio gemello/la mia gemella.	*KWELL-oh/ah AIR-ah eel MEE-oh jay-MELL-oh/lah MEE-ah jay-MELL-ah.*
He's/she's out of town this week.	È fuori città questa settimana.	*Ay FWOR-ee chee-TAH KWEST-ah SET-ee-MON-ah.*
I'll have him/her call you when he/she returns.	La farò chiamare quando ritorna.	*La far-OH kyah-MAR-ay KWON-doh ree-TORN-ah.*
Yes, of course, I'll tell him/her to drive more carefully.	Si, naturalmente. Gli/Le dirò di guidare più prudentemente.	*See, NOT-ur-ahl-MENT-ay. Lyee/Lay deer-OH dee gwee-DAR-ay pyu pru-DENT-eh-MENT-ay.*

DRIVE AND SURVIVE

ROAD SIGNS

All motorists must learn to decipher basic road signs. But there are many obscure international symbols that alert the astute driver to cultural hazards and opportunities.

PICTURESQUE
OLD MEN
AHEAD

OUTRAGEOUS
PRICES
NEXT 20 KM

SLOW DOWN–
SAINT'S TEETH

VIRGIN
500 METERS

WARNING:
HORNY MEN
NEXT 10 KM

SHOUTING IN TRAFFIC

An *epiteto* (epithet) is satisfying only if the intended victim understands it. Visiting drivers may start their own authentic Italian shouting matches with these phrases.

(Note: Italian tempers are not just the stuff of legend; they are real. Before using these lines, lock the doors and put your vehicle in gear.)

What a jerk!	Che stupido!	*Kay STOO-pee-doh!*
What are you? Crazy?	Ma è pazzo?	*May ay POT-soh?*
Move that junk pile, you cretin!	Muova quel rottame, cretino!	*Moo-OH-vah kwell roh-TOM-ay, cray-TEEN-oh!*
You drive like a ninety-year-old woman!	Guida come una novantenne!	*GWEE-dah COH-may OON-ah NO-von-TEN-ay!*
Have you swallowed your brain?	Si è bevuto il cervello?	*See ay bay-VOOT-oh eel chair-VELL-oh?*
Maybe they will teach you to drive in hell.	Speriamo che all'inferno le insegnino a guidare.	*SPARE-ee-YOM-oh kay ahl-in-FAIRN-oh lay in-SANE-yair-ON-oh ah gwee-DAR-ay.*

BEAUTIFUL NAMES OF REVOLTING DISHES AND VICE VERSA

Italian chefs have some unattractive names for wonderful dishes. *Pasta alla puttanesca*, for example, means "spaghetti of the slut," so called because it doesn't require hours in the kitchen. *Saltimbocca*, a classic Roman dish that translates as "jump in the mouth," is sliced veal with Marsala, ham, and sage. *Zuppa dei poveri*, "soup of the poor," is a hearty mixture of greens, oil, cheese, and stale bread.

Just as great dishes may have unfortunate names, revolting dishes may sound delicious. Even astute travelers can be fooled. Those with delicate sensibilities should take note of the following phrases, in order to recognize and decline alien entrées. (Euphemism has been eliminated in the English phrases.)

Please cut the head off.	Per piacere, mi tagli la testa.	*Pair-pee-ah-CHAIR-ay, mee TAL-yee lah TASTE-ah.*
Excuse me, but which organs are these?	Scusi, ma che organi sono questi?	*SKOO-see, mah kay OR-gan-ee SO-noh KWEST-ee?*

Thank you, but I had blood pudding for breakfast.	Grazie, ma ho già avuto il sanguinaccio per prima colazione	*GROT-zee-ay, mah oh jah ah-VOOT-oh eel sahn-gwee-NAHCH-choh pair PREE-mah coh-LATS-ee-OWN-ay.*
I'm violently allergic to pickled eels.	Sono davvero allergico/a alle anguille sotto aceto.	*SO-noh da-VAIR-oh ah-LAIR-jee-coh/cah AH-lay on-GWEEL-ay SOTE-oh ah-CHET-oh.*
Also to stewed frogs and reptiles of any kind.	E anche agli stufati di rane e rettili di ogni genere.	*Ay ONK-ay AHL-yee stoo-FOT-ee dee RAH-nay ay RAY-tee-lee dee OWN-yee JEN-air-ay.*
The rabbit smothered in bitter chocolate sounds a bit heavy.	La lepre piemontese mi risulta un po' pesante.	*Lah LEP-ray PEE-moan-TAZE-ay mee ree-SOOLT-ah oon poe pay-ZONT-ay.*
You're out of grilled lamb's guts?	No ha più nessuna cordula?	*Noan ah pyu nay-SOON-ah core-DOOL-ah?*
What a pity! Perhaps the brain with capers, then.	Che peccato! Allora, cervella con i capperi.	*Kay pay-COT-oh! Ah-LORE-ah, chair-VELL-ah cone ee ca-PAIR-ay.*

DECLINING THE IMPERATIVE

talian cooks may be genuinely hurt when guests cannot eat everything they serve. They don't realize that people in other civilizations consume less than their own weight at mealtime.

When you've had your fill, you can help a cook preserve her respect for you and for herself with a few carefully chosen phrases.

This is the best food I have ever tasted in my life.	Questo è il miglior cibo che abbia mai assaggiato.	KWEST-oh ay eel MEAL-yore CHEE-boh kay AH-bee-yah my ah-sah-JAH-toh.
I am your slave.	Sono il tuo schiavo.	SO-noh eel TOO-oh ski-OV-oh.
This meal has given me metric tons of joy, but I'm stuffed to the gills.	Questo pasto mi ha dato riempito di gioia, ma sono pieno fin sopra i capelli.	KWEST-oh PAH-stoh me ah DOT-oh ree-aym-PEE-toh dee JOY-ah, ma SO-noh pee-EN-oh feen SOAP-rah ee cah-PELL-ee.
No more food.	Non datemi nient'altro da mangiare.	Noan DOT-ay-me nee-EN-TAL-troh da mon-JAR-ay.
Please call an ambulance.	Chiami un ambulanza, per piacere.	Key-AH-mee oon Am-bew-LON-zah, pair pya-CHAIR-ay.

SECRETS OF THE ITALIAN COFFEE SHOP

Prices in a *bar*, or coffee shop, differ depending on the customer's posture and geographical location. Plumbing the mysteries of this pricing system requires four simple questions.

How much is coffee standing up?	Quanto è il caffè al banco?	*KWON-toh ay eel cah-FAY-all BONK-oh?*
How much if I sit here by the bar?	Quanto è al tavolino?	*KWON-toh ay all TAH-voh-LEEN-oh?*
How much seated on the terrace?	E quanto sulla terrazza?	*Ay KWON-toh SOOL-ah tare-OTZ-ah?*
How much in the restaurant next door?	E quanto al ristorante accanto?	*Ay KWON-toh all REEST-oh-RONT-ay ah CON-toh?*

MEANINGFUL THINGS TO SAY ABOUT OLIVE OIL

O live oil, the foundation of nearly all Italian cooking, can lubricate a conversation as well as a saucepan. The very best Italian oil is so delicious that philosophers have cited it as proof of the existence of God. Italians take olive oil as seriously as the French do wine, and an ability to comment on olive oil is a sign of sophistication.

This olive oil has a subtle, sweet virginity.	Questo olio d'oliva è di una verginità molto sottile, molto dolce.	*KWEST-oh OH-leo doe-LEE-vah ay dee OON-ah vair-JEEN-ee-TAH MOLE-toh soh-TEEL-ay, MOLE-toh DOLE-chay.*
One taste tells you the olives grew in full view of the cathedral.	Se lo assaggia capisce che le olive sono maturate di fronte ad una cattedrale.	*Say loh ah-SAH-jah kah-PEE-shay kay lay oh-LEE-vay SO-noh MAH-too-ROT-ay dee FRONE-tay ad OON-ah COT-ay-DRAHL-ay.*
They were hand-picked by the Blind Nuns of Tuscany.	Sono state raccolte dalle suore cieche della Toscana.	*SO-noh STAH-tay rah-COLT-ay DAH-lay SWORE-ay CHECK-ay DELL-ah toe-SKAH-nah.*

And cold-pressed just before puberty.	Sono state spremute appena prima della pubertà.	*SO-noh STAH-tay spray-MOOT-ay ah-PAIN-ah PREE-mah DELL-ah POO-bare-TAH.*
Wait until you taste the extra virgin!	Ma aspetta di assaggiare quello extra vergine!	*Mah ah-SPETT-ah-dee AH-sah-JAR-ay KWELL-oh EX-trah VAIR-jeen-ay.*

YOUR INEVITABLE STAINS

Every restaurant in Italy stocks a bottle of *borotalco* (unscented talc) with which to dust olive oil stains. Seasoned travelers can tell what a person had for dinner according to the size, shape, and location of his or her talc marks. Long pastas such as spaghetti can fling oil for several feet, leaving welt-like marks from collar to cuff. Short pastas tend to drop and stick, leaving their unmistakable impressions on and about the thigh region. Slippery, round pastas such as rigatoni tend to drop and roll, leaving the ever-popular *linea incisa* (hatch mark) and classic *ellissi* (ellipses).

YOUR MEDICAL EMERGENCY

E xplaining ailments to foreign doctors is never
easy, and covering all medical terminology is
beyond the scope of this book. Phrases are
provided for a restaurant setting, where Italian
medical emergencies are most likely to occur.

Is there a doctor in the house?	C'è un dottore in casa?	*Chay ooon doe-TORE-ay een CAH-zah?*
I don't know what's wrong.	Non capisco cos'è che non va.	*Noan cah-PEACE-coh coze-AY kay noan vah.*
He started drinking the olive oil straight from the bottle.	Lui si è attaccato alla bottiglia dell'olio d'oliva.	*LOO-ee see ay at-ah-COT-oh AH-lah boh-TEEL-yah dell-OH-leo doe-LEE-vah.*
Then he fell over unconscious.	Poi ha perso i sensi.	*Poy ah PAIR-soh ee SEN-see.*
Yes, it certainly is good oil. Extra virgin.	Sì, è certamente un buon olio. Extra vergine.	*See, ay CHAIR-tah-MENT-ay oon bwone OH-leo. EX-trah VAIR-jeen-ay.*
Perhaps that is why he is still smiling.	Forse quella è la ragione per cui sorride.	*FOR-zay KWELL-ah ay lah rah-ZONE-ay pair kwee soh-REE-day.*

Is that fork sterile?	Questa forchetta è sterilizzata?	*KWEST-ah for-CHET-ah ay STAIR-ah-lee-ZOT-ah?*
When should I remove the leeches?	Quando posso rimuovere le sanguisughe?	*KWON-doh POE-soh ree-MWOH-vair-ay lay sahng-gwee-SOOG-ay?*
I'm afraid I don't have that much cash at the moment.	Mi dispiace, ma al momento non ho tutto questo contante.	*Me DEE-spee-YOTCH-ay, mah al mo-MENT-oh noan oh TOOT-oh KWEST-oh con-TONT-ay.*
Perhaps you could mail me your bill.	Forse può spedirmi il conto.	*FOR-say pwoh sped-EAR-me eel CONE-toh.*
Isn't it too early to administer last rites?	Crede sia troppo presto per l'estrema unzione?	*CRAY-do SEE-ah TROH-poh PREST-oh pair les-TRAY-mah oon-zee-OWN-ay?*
Okay, okay, I'll pay up!	Va bene, va bene, pagherò!	*Vah BANE-ay, vah BANE-ay, pah-gare-OH!*
I didn't know you accepted MasterCard.	Non sapevo che accettavate la MasterCard.	*Noan say-PAY-voh kay ah-CHET-ah-VOT-ay la Mastercard.*

THE SHOE AND THE WALLET

Italy is the undisputed arbiter of style in *scarpe* (footwear). Italian cobblers create shoes from the skins of an incredible variety of organisms. You're sure to want a pair.

Dealing with shoe salespeople requires a few simple phrases.

Those crocodile loafers are stupendous.	Quelle pantofole di coccodrillo sono stupende.	*KWELL-ay pan-TOH-foh-lay dee COKE-oh-DREEL-oh SO-noh stoo-PEND-ay.*
I had better buy a pair before they're extinct.	Meglio che ne prenda un paio prima che finiscano.	*MAIL-yo kay nay PREND-ah oon PIE-yo PREE-mah kay fee-NEE-scah-noh.*
Do you have them in another color?	Ne ha di un altro colore?	*Nay ah dee oon AHL-troh coh-LORE-ay?*
The pale blue clashes with my slacks.	Il celeste stona con i miei pantaloni.	*Eel chay-LEST-ay STONE-ah cone ee me-AY PONT-ah-LONE-ee*
I'll take them. How much are they?	Le prendo. A proposito, quanto costano?	*Lay PREND-oh. Ah proh-POH-see-toh, KWON-toh COAST-ah-noh?*

Could I have some water?	Potrei avere un po' d'acqua?	*Poh-TRAY ah-VAIR-ay oon poh DOCK-wah?*
My credit card is on fire.	La mia carta di credito si è incendiata.	*Lah ME-ah CART-ah dee CRAY-dee-toh see ay in-SEND-ee-AH-tah.*

PRAYER TO SAINT FERRAGAMO

Oh Saint Ferragamo, Precious Cobbler to the Stars, Gifted Designer of Soles, grant me just one pair of those open-heeled high heels I saw in the window tonight, the purple ones. Size six would be perfect, Blessed Hooved One.

O San Ferragamo, Calzolaio Prezioso alle Stelle, Stilista Dotato di Suole, concedimi un paio di quelle scarpe tipo chanel a tacco alto che ho visto in vetrina questa notte, quelle bordeaux. La misura trentasei sarebbe perfetta, Siano Benedetti i Portatori de Zoccoli.

SHOPPING AND SIGHTSEEING

ARMANI VERSUS OUR MONEY

I talian men's clothing is at the cutting edge of fashion and price. But even if you can afford it, a good Italian suit is simply too stylish unless you are slim, live in Manhattan, and use expensive gels. People caught wearing Versace in Cincinnati usually spend the night in jail.

Nevertheless, trying on suits in a sleek little Italian shop is an entertaining way to waste a salesman's valuable time.

Wow. This suit is divine.	Wow. Questo vestito è divino.	*Wow. KWEST-oh ves-TEET-oh ay dee-VEEN-oh.*
Could I get wider lapels on the jacket?	Posso avere il risvolto della giacca più grande?	*POE-soh ah-VAIR-ay eel reez-VOLT-oh DELL-ah JOCK-ah pyu GRON-deh?*
I'd like them to meet in back.	Vorrei che si congiungessero dietro.	*Vore-AY kay see kon-joon-JESS-air-oh dee-AY-troh.*
Ah! This duffel bag matches the suit.	Ah! Questa sacca si intona con il vestito.	*Ah! KWEST-ah SOCK-ah see een-TONE-ah cone eel ves-TEET-oh.*

Oh, this isn't a duffel bag. This is a pair of pants.	Oh, non è una sacca. Sono dei pantaloni.	*Oh, noan ay OON-ah SOCK-ah. SO-noh day PONT-ah-LONE-ee.*
I could never wear this suit in Midland.	Non potrei mai portare questo vestito a Midland.	*Noan poe-TRAY my por-TAH-ray KWEST-oh ves-TEET-oh ah MEED-lon.*
But I'd love to wear it around Rome.	Ma sarebbe stupendo portarlo in giro per Roma.	*Mah sah-RAY-bay stoo-PEND-oh por-TAR-loh in JEER-oh pair ROME-ah.*
Could I rent it?	Posso noleggiarlo?	*POE-soh no-lay-JAR-loh?*

UNDERSTANDING ITALIAN BUSINESS HOURS

Everyone knows Italians keep schedules that are different from ours. The Wicked Traveler knows how they actually fill those schedules.

	WHAT THEY'RE DOING	WHAT'S HAPPENING TO YOU
MORNING		
8:00	Fondling Spouse.	Woken by disturbing noises.
9:00	Shooting espresso.	Woken by maid.
10:00	On the phone at work, making "lunch" plans.	Line at bank is even wider than it is long.
11:00	Discussing opposite sex with fellow employee.	Car rental clerks chatter endlessly among themselves.
12:00	Pre-lunch grooming.	Pharmacist invisible.
AFTERNOON		
1:00	Racing to arms of lover.	Museum closed for "lunch."
2:00	Consuming enormous amounts of food.	Restaurant has stopped serving.
3:00	Even more food.	Egg salad sandwich.
4:00	Cappuccino in café.	Meet charming stranger in café. Campari begins taking effect.

SHOPPING AND SIGHTSEEING

EVENING

5:00	Strolling back to work.	Meet charming stranger on street.
6:00	Sweet-talking spouse by phone.	Make eyes with bartender, who is on the phone.
7:00	Changing clothes at home. Family shouting match.	Campari recharge is effective, but charming strangers are gone.
8:00	Meeting lover.	Restaurant filled with tourists.
9:00	Strolling along river.	Make eyes with charming strollers.
10:00	Quiet dinner at home.	Streets deserted.

LATE EVENING

11:00	Fondling spouse.	Return to hotel. Odd cooing sounds from other rooms.
12:00	Retiring to separate bedroom to read.	Practice Italian for next day's adventures.
1:00	Well-earned sleep.	Well-earned sleep.

SOLVING THE RIDDLE OF MUSEUM HOURS

The museum hours published in guide books are almost totally useless. If a museum *chiude* (closes) at 1:00 P.M., it means that at 12:45 the building will be empty and the employees will already be home eating lunch. Of course, there will never be a schedule for strikes, renovations, whims, or acts of God.

Why is the museum closed today?	Ma perché il museo è chiuso oggi?	*Mah pair-KAY eel moo-ZAY-oh ay CUE-soh OH-jee?*
Who the hell is Saint Fiammetta?	Chi diavolo è Santa Fiammetta?	*Key dee-AH-voh-loh ay SAHN-tah fee-ah-MET-ah?*
One ecstatic vision and she gets a national holiday?	Una sola visione estatica ed ha avuto un giorno festivo nazionale?	*OON-ah SO-lah VEEZ-ee-OWN-ay ay-STOT-ee-kah aid ah ah-VOOT-oh oon JOR-noh fest-EE-voh NOTS-ee-oh-NAL-ay?*
Why is the museum closed tomorrow?	Ma perché il museo è chiuso domani?	*Mah pair-KAY eel moo-ZAY-oh ay CUE-soh doh-MAH-nee?*

SHOPPING AND SIGHTSEEING

How long will they be on strike?	Quanto tempo staranno in sciopero?	*KWON-toh TEMP-oh star-ON-oh een SHOW-pair-oh?*
Is it true that the renovation began in 1954?	È vero che il restauro è cominciato nel millenovecento-cinquantaquattro?	*Ay VAIR-oh kay eel rest-OW-roh ay coh-meen-CHOT-oh nell MEAL-ay-NOVE-ay-CHENT-oh-cheen-KWONT-ah-KWAH-troh?*
Ah, the contractor is the cardinal's nephew!	Oh, l'imprenditore è il nipote del cardinale!	*Oh, lim-PREND-ee-TORE-ay ay eel nee-POTE-ay dell car-dee-NAL-ay!*
We just want to see the Madonna.	Vogliamo soltanto vedere la Madonna.	*Vole-YAH-moh sole-TONT-oh vay-DARE-ay lah mah-DOAN-ah.*
I've never seen a Michelangelo.	Non ho mai visto un Michelangelo.	*No hoh my VEEST-oh oon MEEK-el-AN-jello.*
Please. We're in love.	Per favore. Siamo innamorati.	*Pair fah-VORE-ay. See-YA-mo EEN-ah-more-AH-tee.*
Oh, thank you so much. We'll never forget you.	Oh, grazie mille. Non la dimenticheremo mai.	*Oh, GROT-zee-ay MEAL-ay. Noan lah dee-MENT-ee-care-AY-moh my.*

YOUR EMERGENCY CONFESSION

Nearly everyone who visits Italy looks into a cathedral or two. But in admiring the art and architecture alone, many people miss the fact that these are working churches with clergy and congregations. Visitors should be warned, however, that Italian priests are very different from the ones at home. Many of them admire adult women, for example. If you wish to make a confession, here are a few phrases worth knowing.

Forgive me father, for I have sinned.	Mi perdoni padre, perché ho peccato.	*Mee-pair-DOAN-ee PAH-dray, pair-KAY oh pay-COT-oh.*
It has been two hours/days/ weeks/months/ years since my last confession.	Sono passati due ore/giorni/ settimane/mesi/ anni dalla mia ultima confessione.	*SO-noh pah-SOT-ee DOO-ay ORE-ay/ JOR-nee/SET-ee- MON-ay/MAY-zee/ ON-ee DAH-lah MEE- ah OOL-teem-ah con- FESS-ee-OWN-AY.*
I've made love to six women/men since my arrival.	Dal mio arrivo ho fatto l'amore con sei donne/uomini.	*Doll MEE-oh ah- REEV-oh oh FAH-toh lah-MORE-ay cone SAY DOAN-ay/ WHOA-me-nee.*

RELIGION, POLITICS, AND SPORTS

Yesterday.	Ieri.	*Ee-AIR-ee.*
I didn't come here to be congratulated, father.	Non sono venuto qui per ricevere delle congratulazioni, padre.	*Noan SO-noh vay-NOOT-oh kwee pair ree-CHAY-vair-ay DELL-ay con-GRAH-too-LOT-zee-OWN-ee, PAH-dray.*
Two Hail Marys is a little light, don't you think?	Due Ave Maria sono un po' poco, non crede?	*DOO-ay AH-vay mah-REE-ah SO-noh oon poh POH-coh, noan CRAY-day?*
How about a couple of Our Fathers, too?	Piuttosto due Padre Nostro?	*Pyu TOAST-oh DOO-ay PAH-dray NO-stroh?*
Thank you, father.	Grazie, padre.	*GROT-zee-ay, PAH-dray.*
But I'm busy this evening.	Ma sono impegnato questa sera.	*Mah SO-noh EEM-pain-YOT-oh KWEST-ah SAIR-ah.*
Is tomorrow night good?	Domani sera andrebbe bene?	*Doh-MON-ee SAIR-ah on-DRAY-bay BANE-ay?*
About eight then?	Alle otto allora?	*AH-lay OAT-oh ah-LORE-ah?*

POLITICAL DISCOURSE

It's usually best to avoid sharing political views in countries where people take these things seriously. Fortunately for those who can't keep their mouths shut, Italy is not one of these places.

Italian politicians hold office so briefly that including names here would be pointless. Instead, general comments are provided.

I love Italian politics!	Adoro la politica italiana!	*Ah-DOOR-oh lah poh-LEE-tee-cah ee-tal-YON-ah!*
Fifty-eight governments since World War II!	Cinquantotto governi dalla seconda guerra mondiale!	*CHEEN-kwan-TOTE-oh go-VAIR-nee DAH-lah say-CONE-dah GWARE-ah moan-dee-AH-lay!*
Cardinals and gangsters vying for political power!	Cardinali e gangster che si contendono il potere politico!	*Car-dee-NAL-ee ay GANG-stair kay see cone-tend-oh-noh eel poh-TARE-ay poh-LEE-tee-co!*
Porno queens in parliament! Great!	E stelle del porno in parlamento! Fantastico!	*Ay STELL-ay dell PORN-oh een PAR-lah-MENT-oh! Fon-TOST-tee-coh!*

RELIGION, POLITICS, AND SPORTS

Workers and intellectuals in the same party!	Operai e intellettuali nello stesso partito!	*OPE-air-ay EEN-tay-LEH-too-AH-lay nelloh STESS-oh por-TEE-toh!*
Just like the old days in my country!	Proprio come ai miei tempi!	*PRO-pree-oh COH-may eye mee-AY TEMP-ee!*
The Italian political system is the world's fairest.	Il sistema politico italiano è il più democratico del mondo.	*Eel sees-TAME-ah poh-LEE-tee-coh ee-tal-YON-oh ay eel pyu day-moh-CROT-ee-coh del MOAN-doh.*
Sooner or later everyone gets to be prime minister, for fifteen minutes.	Tutti prima o poi fanno il primo ministro, per quindici minuti.	*TOOT-ee PREE-mah oh poy FAH-noh eel PREE-moh mee-NEES-stroh, pair KWEEN-deetch-ee mee-NOOT-ee.*

AUTHENTIC SCREAMING FOR SPECTATORS

Italians hate to die on Saturday because it means they have to miss Sunday's *calcio* (soccer) match.

Calcio enthusiasts are loud and obscene, but Italian fans are, by international standards, restrained. They kill fewer than a dozen of their fellows each year.

Visitors who wish to understand what is being shouted at a *calcio* match should study the following phrases.

TO PLAYERS OF THE OPPOSITION:

You sissy!	Frocio!	*FROH-choh!*
Go home to Mommy!	Tornatene dalla mammina!	*TORN-ah-TAY-nay DAH-lah mah-MEAN-ah!*
You play like an old dog!	Giochi come un cane!	*JOKE-ee dah COH-may oon CON-ay!*

TO THE HOME TEAM:

Into the mouth of the wolf!	In bocca al lupo!	*Een-BOKE-ah al LOOP-oh!*
May the wolf die!	Crepi il lupo!	*CRAY-pee eel LOOP-oh!*

RELIGION, POLITICS, AND SPORTS

Up the ass of the whale!	In culo alla balena!	*Een COOL-oh AH-lah bah-LAIN-ah!*
Hope he doesn't fart!	Speriamo che non scoreggi!	*SPARE-ee-YOM-oh kay noan score-EDGE-ee!*

TO THE REFEREES:

Blockhead!	Sei di tek!	*Say dee tek!*
Traitor!	Traditore!	*Trah-dee-TORE-ay!*
Get some glasses!	Mettiti un paio di occhiali!	*Meh-TEE-tee oon PIE-oh dee OAK-ee-AHL-ee!*
Snake!	Serpente!	*Sair-PENT-ay!*
Whose payroll are you on?	Ma chi t'ha pagato?	*Mah key tah pah-GOT-oh?*

MEN: UNLEASH THE LATIN LOVER INSIDE YOU

L ife is short, vacations are shorter, and Italian nights are long. There's no reason to spend them alone. That said, Italian men hate losing their wives and girlfriends, but they can't tolerate losing their honor. Direct your passion carefully.

To compete with the natives, you must know two things: Italian men are willing to exaggerate beyond all bounds of reason, and women are willing to believe them.

Sometimes.

I have never known love until now.	Non ho mai conosciuto l'amore fino ad oggi.	*Noan oh my CONE-oh-SHOOT-oh la-MORE-ay FEEN-oh odd OH-jee.*
The profound mystery of whatever you just said sets my heart on fire.	Il profondo mistero di ciò che stai dicendo mi infuoca il cuore.	*Eel pro-FOND-oh mee-STAIR-oh dee cho kay sty dee-CHEND-oh me een-FWOKE-ah eel KWORE-ay.*
I will kill myself if you ever leave me.	Se mi lasci mi uccido.	*Say mee LOSH-ee mee oo-CHEE-doh.*

What is your name, my celestial fruit basket?	Come ti chiami, mio cestino di frutta celestiale?	*COH-may tee KYAH-mee, MEE-oh chess-TEEN-oh dee FROOT-ah chay-LESS-tee-AL-ay?*
Your name is like an ageless aria to my ears.	Il tuo nome suona alle mie orecchie come una melodia senza età.	*Eel TOO-oh NOH-may SWONE-ah AH-lay MEE-ay oh-RECK-ee-ay COH-may OON-ah may-loh-DEE-yah SEN-sah ay-TAH.*
What? This man is your husband?	Che cosa? Quello è tuo marito?!?	*Kay COZE-ah? KWELL-oh ay TOO-oh mah-REET-oh?!?*
You deserve greater joy than such a man could ever provide!	Meriti ben altra gioia che quella che può dare un tipo così!	*MARE-ee-tee bane AHL-trah JOY-ah kay KWELL-ah kay pwoh DAR-ay oon TEEP-oh coh-SEE.*
You deny our everlasting love?	Neghi l'amore eterno?!?	*NEG-ee lah-MORE-ay ay-TAIRN-oh?!?*
Then at least give me your phone number, my heavenly marinara sauce.	Almeno dammi il tuo numero di telefono, mio delizioso sugo alla marinara.	*Ahl-MAIN-oh DAH-mee eel TOO-oh NOOM-air-oh dee tay-LAY-foh-noh, MEE-oh day-leet-SEE-oh-zoh SOOG-oh AH-lah MAR-ee-NAR-ah.*

WOMEN: DEFLATE THE LATIN LOVER BEHIND YOU

An Italian man is unlikely to be dangerous in daylight, but he might act like a caveman in front of (or behind) women he doesn't know personally, particularly those in shorts who have the courage to walk through the streets without a male companion. The wise female visitor arms herself with a few appropriate phrases, a spine-tingling scream, and a large pair of scissors.

Don't touch me.	Non mi tocchi.	*Noan mee TOKE-ee.*
Buzz off, garlic breath.	Vada via che sa di aglio.	*VAH-da VEE-ah kay sah dee AHL-yoh.*
You're disgusting.	Fa schifo.	*Fah SKEE-foh.*
The Sicilian sun has cooked your brain.	Il sole siciliano le ha cotto il cervello.	*Eel SOLE-ay see-cheel-YON-oh lay hah COAT-oh eel chair-VELL-oh.*
Not if you were the last man on earth.	Neanche se lei fosse l'unico uomo sulla terra.	*Nay-ONK-ay say lay FOSS-ay LOON-ee-coh WHOA-moh SOO-lah TAIR-ah.*
Filth!	Sporco!	*SPORE-coh!*

Leave me alone.	Mi lasci in pace.	*Mee LOSH-ee in POTCH-ay.*
You've got a lot of class. Working class.	Lei ha molta classe. Classe proletaria.	*Lay ah MOLE-tah KLOSS-ay. KLOSS-ay PRO-leh-TAR-ee-ah.*
I'll call the police.	Chiamo la polizia.	*KYAH-moh lah poh-leet-SEE-ah.*
Help!	Aiuto!	*Eye-YOU-toh!*

PET NAMES: ANIMAL

A few good *vezzeggiativi* (pet names) add authenticity to an *avventúra* (love affair).

Kitten	*Micio*	*MEECH-oh*
Bunny	*Coniglietto*	*CON-eel-YET-oh*
Duckling	*Paperella**	*PAP-air-ELL-ah*
Little Sparrow	*Passerotto*	*POSS-air-OAT-oh*
Little Mouse	*Topolino*	*TOPE-oh-LEEN-oh*
Little Squirrel	*Scoiattolino*	*skoy-OTT-oh-LEEN-oh*

*refers to women only

THOSE FRIENDLY ITALIANS

MAKING LOVE

The following phrases are provided for the man who wishes to master them, and for the woman who wishes to recognize them.

You look beautiful in the candlelight.	Sei bella al lume di candela.	*Say BELL-ah AH-lah LOO-may dee con-DEL-ah.*
You must be even more beautiful in the dark.	Devi essere più bella nell'oscurità.	*DAY-vee ESS-air-ay pyu BELL-ah nell oh-SKOOR-ee-TAH.*
Would you like a Campari/some Chianti?	Gradisci un Campari/Chianti?	*Gra-DEESH-ee oon com-PAR-ee/kee YONT-ee?*
Will you join me for dinner?	Verresti a cena con me?	*Vay-REST-ee ah CHAIN-ah cone may?*
My wife is very fat, and has many warts.	Mia moglie è grassissima ed è piena di porri.	*MEE-ah MOLE-yay ay gra-SEES-ee-mah aid ay pee-EN-ah dee PORR-ee.*
She no longer loves me.	Non mi ama più.	*Noan mee AH-mah pyu.*

PET NAMES: VEGETABLE

LIttle Sugar	*Zuccherino*	*ZOOK-air-EEN-oh*
LIttle Sweetie	*Dolcezza*	*dole-CHETS-ah*
Little Cookie	*Biscottino*	*BEESK-oh-TEEN-oh*
Little Strawberry	*Fragolina**	*FROG-oh-LEAN-ah*

*refers to women only

Dinner was delicious. What's for dessert?	La cena era squisita. Cosa c'è per dessert?	*Lah CHAIN-ah AIR-ah SQUEEZE-ee-tah. COZE-ah chay pair dess-AIRT?*
Would you like to see my sculptures?	Ti piacerebbe vedere le mie sculture?	*Tee pee-OTCH-air-ABE-ay vay-DARE-ay lay MEE-ay skool-TURE-ay?*
May I show you my obelisk?	Posso mostrarti il mio obelisco?	*POE-soh moh-STRAR-tee eel MEE-oh OH-bay-LEES-coh?*
Take off your clothes.	Spogliati.	*SPOLE-yah-tee.*
Take off my clothes.	Spogliami.	*SPOLE-yah-mee.*

(continued)

THOSE FRIENDLY ITALIANS

You are very beautiful.	Sei molto bella.	*Say MOLE-toh BELLA-ah.*
Your breasts are like melons from Tuscany.	Il tuo seno è come i meloni toscani.	*Eel TOO-oh SANE-oh ay COH-may ee may-LONE-ee toe-SKAH-nee.*
Hug me.	Abbracciami.	*Ah-BROTCH-ah-mee.*
Kiss me.	Baciami.	*BOTCH-ah-mee.*
My treasure.	Tesoro mio.	*Tay-ZORE-oh MEE-oh.*
Slower.	Più piano.	*Pyu pee-AH-noh.*
Faster.	Più in fretta.	*Pyu een FRETT-ah.*
Oh my God.	Oh mio Dio.	*Oh MEE-oh DEE-oh.*
I love you.	Ti amo.	*Tee ah-moh*
I will never leave you.	Non ti lascerò mai.	*Noan tee LOSH-air-OH my*
Shall we pray?	Preghiamo?	*PRESG-ee-AH-moh?*
Heavenly Father, let me fall asleep now and wake up an Italian. Amen.	Dio del Paradiso, fa che adesso mi addormenti e che mi possa svegliare italiano. Così sia.	*DEE-oh dell para-DEE-soh, fay kay ah-DESS-oh mee AH-dor-MENT-ee ay kay mee POE-sah SVELL-ee-AH-ray ee-TAHL-ee-AH-no. coh-SEE SEE-ah.*

DENYING YOUR INFIDELITY

J ealousy plays a leading role in Italian romance and comes naturally to those not inclined to strict fidelity. Any tourist lucky enough to get embroiled in Italian romance will need a few bold-faced lies.

Here are some flowers.	Ecco dei fiori.	*ECK-oh day fee-ORE-ee.*
Sorry I'm late.	Scusa il ritardo.	*SCOO-sah eel ree-TARD-oh.*
But I love only you, my sweet.	Ma amo solo te, dolcezza mia.	*Mah AH-moh SO-loh tay, dole-CHETS-ah-MEE-ah.*
What are you talking about?	Che stai dicendo?	*Kay sty dee-CHEND-oh?*
Her/Him? Don't make me laugh.	Lei/Lui? Ma non formi ridere.	*LAY/LOO-ee? Mah noan FAHR-mee REED-air-ay.*
I could never love a woman/man like her/him.	Non potrei mai amare una donna/ un uomo come lei/lui.	*Noan po-TRAY my ah-MAR-ay OON-ah DOAN-ah/oon WHOA-moh COH-may LAY/LOO-ee.*
She/He is twenty years younger/older than I am!	Ha vent'anni meno/più di me!	*Ah vain-TAH-nee MAY-noh/pyu dee may!*

(continued)

THOSE FRIENDLY ITALIANS

Her breasts are much too large for my taste.	Le sue tette sono troppo grandi per i miei gusti.	*Lay SOO-ay TET-ay SO-noh TROH-poh GRON-dee, pair ee mee-AY GOOSE-tee.*
You know I don't like macho men.	Lo sai che non mi piacciono i maschioni.	*Loh sigh kay noan mee pee-OTCH-oh-noh ee MASK-ee-OWN-ee.*
Besides, she/he is married.	Per di più è sposato/a	*Pair dee pyu ay spo-ZOT-oh/ah.*
You're imagining things.	Tu sogni.	*Too SOAN-yee.*

PET NAMES: CELESTIAL

My Soul	*Anima Mia*	*Ah-ee-mah MEE-ah*
My Love	*Amore Mio*	*ah-MORE-ay MEE-oh*
Treasure	*Tesoro*	*tay-ZORE-oh*
Angel	*Angelo*	*Ah-jell-oh*

EFFECTIVE LETTER-WRITING

S easoned tourists always send *biglietti di grazie* (thank-you notes) to their hosts and drop cards to people they meet during their adventures. These are the travelers who are invited to stay in the home of natives. They have richer cultural experiences and lower hotel bills.

Many Italians carry calling cards and will be flattered if you ask for one.

Letters and postcards are more effective when the author makes a sincere attempt to use the native language. The following are phrases commonly needed in this type of correspondence.

Dear John/Martha,	Caro/a Giovanni/Martina,
It was a great pleasure to meet you.	È stato un vero piacere incontrarti.
Your entire family is wonderful.	Tutta la tua famiglia è fantastica.
I've never heard so much shouting!	Non ho mai sentito urlare così tanto!
I admire the Italian passion for debate.	Ammiro la passione italiana per le discussioni.
Sorry about the tomato sauce episode.	Mi dispiace per l'incidente della pommarola.

(continued)

THOSE FRIENDLY ITALIANS

I hope the stains come out.	Spero che le macchie siano venute via.
That grappa was the smoothest rocket fuel I've ever tasted.	Quella grappa era il carburante più morbido che abbia mai assaggiato.
Sorry if my pope jokes offended anyone.	Scusami, se il mio scherzo sul papa ha offeso qualcuno.
I admit that the one about the blind virgin was in poor taste.	Ammetto che quello sulla vergine cieca era di cattivo gusto.
Sorry about your parents/ husband catching us in the act.	Mi dispiace che i tuoi genitori/tuo marito ci abbiano/ci abbia sorpreso sul più bello.
By the way, you'll soon be a father/I don't believe the baby is mine.	A proposito, presto sarai padre/non credo che il bambino sia mio.
I miss you very much.	Mi manchi tanto.
But it's over between us.	Ma è finita tra di noi.
Yours truly, (Your name)	Caramente, (Your name)

Wicked
JAPANESE

Kazoku sorrote no seppuku ga yokatta.

I loved the part where the whole family disemboweled themselves.

Kah-ZOH-koo soh-ROH-teh no say-POO-koo ga yoh-KAH-tah.

CONTENTS

SOCIAL JAPAN

WORKING FOR THE JAPANESE

STALKING THE DEAL

MYSTERY AND MASTERY

F ew Westerners visit Japan for pleasure. It's farther away than Fiji, more crowded than New York, more expensive than surgery, and more alien than Mars.

To be sure, the country offers many exotic thrills, such as the chance to eat endangered species, worship at a shrine devoted to sex organs, or pay vast sums to sleep on the floor.

But Japan isn't simply an odd version of what we're used to, like Canada. Thanks to centuries of isolation, the Japanese have developed unique approaches to everything from architecture, music, and haircuts to the meaning of silence.

For centuries, visitors have found it difficult to adapt to Japanese culture, so they tend to visit the island nation only when they have a really good reason, such as making money. This book is meant to help readers return home not just with happy memories and interesting snapshots, but also with clear understandings and signed contracts.

The arcane world of Japanese business requires a lot from Westerners who would attempt to plumb its mysteries and make a profit. Careful verbal and emotional preparation is required because many of the qualities we admire in our salespeople and executives—charm, candor, aggressiveness, unusual neckties—spell disaster in Japan.

There isn't enough room here to get to the bottom of every mystery, such as why people who are so elaborately polite will urinate in the street, why they admire and despise us so deeply, or how they make some of the finest products on earth without paying their chief executives more than $20 million a year.

This book is meant to help foster in Wicked Businesspeople the basic skills they need to get in, have some fun, win a couple of financial swordfights, and get the hell out.

Banzai!

INSTANT TRANSLATION GUIDE

Hundreds of English words have entered Japanese, modified to suit the Japanese tongue. Many come from Hollywood, whose products have penetrated even the most protected markets. There are two basic rules for proper pronunciation: consonants are always separated by a vowel, and the sounds "r" and "l" are indistinguishable. With these rules, you can translate any English phrase into "Japlish."

Here are some classic examples.

hostess	*hosu-tesu*
beer	*beeru*
salary man	*sarariman*
nice little girl	*nigh-su ree-tu gee-aru*
hot	*hot-toh*
enormous	*ah-nolo-moo-su*
lollipop	*roh-ree poppu*
love hotel	*rabu hoteru*
Lolita complex	*rorita compa-rekusu*

THE FOUR MAJOR BELIEF SYSTEMS: BUDDHISM, SHINTO, LIFO AND FIFO

The underlying philosophies that guide our lives are alien to Japanese thinking, including the concepts of good and evil, right and wrong, and generally accepted accounting principles. As a result, the Japanese feel comfortable subscribing to many beliefs simultaneously.

The following phrases will help you join the discussion at religious or business meetings.

BUDDHISM			
Why does the lotus bloom?	Hasu no hana ga saku, sono imi wa ikani?	ハスの花が咲く、その意味はいかに？	*Ha-soo no HA-na ga SA-koo so-no EE-mee wa ee-CON-ee?*
What is the meaning of my belly-button?	Ohesotte nani?	おヘソって何？	*Oh-hay-so-tay nak-NEE?*
Where does all the money go?	Kono okane wa donaru no desuka?	このお金はどうなるのですか？	*KO-no oh-CON-ay wa doe-NAH-roo no DESK-ah?*

(continued)

SHINTO

Always be sure to please the gods.	Itsumo kamigami no ini shitagau—beshi.	いつも神々の意に従うべし。	*ITS-mo KAH-me-GA-mee no EE-nee shee-TAG-ah oo-BESH-ee.*
When you have time.	Sonna hima ga attara ne.	そんな暇があったらね。	*So-nah HEE-ma ga AH-tah-rah nay.*
If you believe or not.	Shinjite iyoto, shinjite imaito.	信じていようと、信じていまいと。	*Shin-JEE-teh ee-YO-toh, shin-Jee-teh EE-ma-EE-toh.*

LIFO

Catch up and pass (the West)!	Oitsuke oikose (seiyo ni)!	追いつけ、追いこせ（西洋に）！	*Oh-eet-SOO-kay oh-ee-KO-say (SAY-oh nee)!*
Forget your wife and children.	Tsuma ya kodomo o wasure nasai.	妻や子供を忘れなさい。	*Tsoo-ma ya ko-DOH-mo oh wa-soo-ray na-SIGH.*
Follow the hierarchy or get squashed like the October plum.	Soshiki ni shitagawa naito, umeboshi mitai ni hosareru yo.	組織に従わないと、梅干しみたいに干されるよ。	*So-SHEE-kee nee shee-tah-GA-wah na-EE-toh, oo-may-BOH-shee me-TAI nee HOH-sah-RAY-roo yoh.*

FIFO

Make GNP swell like belly of your wife!	Anta no okusan no onaka mitaini GNP o fukurama se yo!	あんたの奥さんのお腹みたいにGNPをふくらませよう！	*AHN-ta no OAK-san meet-ah-EE-nee gee en pee oh foo-koo RA-ma say yo!*
Make production flow like a mountain stream.	Nagareru keiryu no yoni mono o seisan shitsuzukeyo.	流れる渓流の様に物を生産し続けよう。	*Nah-ga-RAY-roo KAY-roo no YOH-nee MOH-no o say-san sheet-soo-zoo-KAY-oh.*
Vacation is for hooligans and foreigners soft as sashimi.	Kyuka wa namakemono to sashimi mitaini yawana gaijin no kangaeru koto da.	休暇はナマケ者と刺身みたいにやわな外人の考える事だ。	*Key-OO-kah wah NA-ma-kay-MOH-no toh sa-SHEE-mee MEET-ah-EE-nee ya-WAH-nah GUY-jeen no KON-gah-AY-roo KOH-toh da.*

QUOTE THE MASTERS

The Japanese love pithy sayings and seem to have one for every occasion. The most ancient of these sayings are Chinese, reflecting Japan's real philosophical heritage. Conversationalists should have a few aphorisms memorized to make points and conclude discussions.

	CONFUCIUS (551–479 B.C.)		
Four words the Master forbids: *certainly, shall, must* and *I.*	Yottsu no kinku: kakujitsuni, zettai, nebanaranai, watashiga.	四つの禁句： 確実に、絶対、 ねばならない、 私が。	*YOTE-soo no KEEN-koo: KAH-koo-jeet-soo-nee zet-TAI, NAY-bah-NAH-rah-NAI, WAH-tah-SHEE-gah.*
Four words the Master likes very much: *perhaps, maybe, possibly* and *later.*	Yottsu no yoi kotoba: moshikashite, tabun, kamoshirenai, atode.	四つの 良い言葉： もしかして、 多分、かもし れない、あとで。	*YOTE-soo no yoy KOH-toh-BAH: MOSH-kah-shee-TEH, tah-BUN, KAH-moh-SHEE-ren-AI, ah-TOE-day.*

MENG-TSE (372–289? B.C.)

He who drives well but putts poorly is like a brutish animal.	Doraibu wa yoikedo patto ga hetana hito wa araarashii yaju to onaji da.	ドライブは良いけどパットが下手な人は、荒々しい野獣と同じだ。	*Doh-RAI-boo wa YOH-ee-kay-DOH PAH-toh ga hay-TAH-nah HEE-toh wa ah-RAH-rah-SHEE yah-joo toh oh-NAH-jee dah.*
He who putts well but drives poorly loses many balls.	Patto wa yoiga doraibu ga hetana hito wa ushinau boru ga oi.	パットは良いがドライブが下手な人は失うボールが多い。	*PAH-toh wa yoh-EE-gah doh-RAI-boo ga hay-TAH-nah HEE-toh wa OO-shee-now BOH-roo ga OH-ee.*
He who drives poorly and putts poorly should take up ikebana (flower arranging).	Doraibu mo patto mo hetana hitoniwa ikebana ga aru.	ドライブもパットも下手な人には活花がある。	*Doh-RAI-boo mo PAH-toh mo hay-TAH-nah HEE-toh-NEE-wah ee-KAY-bah-nah ga AH-roo.*

FOR WOMEN ONLY

In Japan as elsewhere, relations between the sexes are complex. Many of the same men who treat women as subhumans give their paychecks to their wives, who make all spending decisions.

After three drinks, men may try to hold an unfamiliar woman's hand or make rude comments while staggering through the streets. A pointed rebuke should stun them into more appropriate behavior.

That is not proper behavior where I come from.	Watashi no kuni dewa souiumane wa shima sen.	私の国では そういう真似は しません。	Wah-TASH-ee no koo-nee DAY-wah so-you-MAH-nay wa shee-MA-sen.
Shame on you!	Haji o shiri nasai!	恥を 知りなさい！	HA-jee oh SHEE-ree nah-SIGH!
Keep your hands to yourself.	Te o shimai nasai.	手を しまいなさい。	Tay oh shee-MY nah-SIGH.
If you want to keep all of your fingers.	Otonashiku shinaito yubi o chongiru wayo.	おとなしく しないと指を ちょん切るわよ。	OH-toh-na-SHEE-koo SHEE-nah-EE-toh Yoo-bee oh chong-EE-roo WHY-oh.

You cold, raw fish without rice!	Sashimi yaro!	さしみ野郎！	*Sah-SHEE-me YAH-roh!*
Get ready to meet your ashamed ancestors!	Anata no gosenzo sama ni kao o awase rare masuka!	あなたの御先祖様に顔を合わせられますか！	*Ah-NAH-ta no goh-SEN-zoh SAH-ma ne kah-OH oh ah-WAH-say RAH-ray mah-soo-kah!*
You'd be no more than a snack for me.	Hashi nimo bo nimo kakara nai wane!	はしにも棒にもかからないわね。	*Hah-shee NEE-moh boh NEE-moh kah-KA-rah nai WAH-nay!*
I'll tear you in half!	Mapputatsuni hiki sakuwayo!	まっぷたつに引き裂くわよ！	*Mah-poo-TOT-soo-nay HEE-kee SAH-koo-WHY-oh!*

OH, NOH!

A s one theatergoer put it, attending a *Noh* play is like being bitten to death by butterflies. The costumes and masks may be fantastic, the stories may be lurid, but the drama disappeared from *Noh* about a thousand years ago.

If you are forced to attend a *Noh* play, try to think of it as meditation rather than punishment. Your invitation to the theater is an honor, and you should be ready to comment on what you have seen.

That was different.	Sozo ijo no mono deshita.	想像以上のものでした。	*Soh-zoh ee-joe no mono desh-tah.*
It was like drops of water boring a hole in my forehead.	Suiteki de atama ni anao akerarete iru yona kokoromochi deshita.	水滴で頭に穴をあけられている様な心持ちでした。	*Soo-ee-TEK-ee day ah-TAH-ma nee ah-NAH-oh AH-kay-ra-RAY-tay EE-roo yoh-na KOH-koh roh-MOH-chee DESH-tah.*
I loved the part where the whole family disemboweled themselves.	Kazoku sorrote no seppuku ga yokatta.	家族そろっての切腹がよかった。	*Kah-ZOH-koo soh-ROH-teh no say-POO-koo ga yoh-KAH-tah.*

How sublime was their suffering!	Karera no kurushimi wa nante totoi mono datta desho!	彼らの 苦しみは何て 尊いものだった でしょう！	*Kah-RAY-rah no koo-roo-SHEE-mee wah NON-tay TOH-toy MOH-noh DAH-tah DAY-sho!*
How gracefully their guts fell to the floor!	Harawata no kobore guai ni hin ga atta!	腹ワタの こぼれ具合に 品があった！	*HAH-rah-WAH-tah no koh-BOH-ray goo-AI nee heen ga AH-tah!*
Their deaths perfectly expressed my deepest desires.	Watashi no nozomi dori no shinikata deshita ne.	私の望み どおりの死に 方でしたね。	*Wah-TAH-shee no noh-ZOH-mee DOH-ree noh SHEE-nee-KAH-tah DESH-tah nay.*

SEVEN REALIZATIONS OF THE SUTRA FOR THE 21st CENTURY

For more than 2000 years, Buddhists have meditated on seven Realizations of the Sutra to escape the cycles of birth and death known as *samsara* and achieve the peace known as *nirvana*.

As Japanese society advances, the Sutra is modified to suit the times.

ANCIENT REALIZATION	MODERN REALIZATION
All material things are impermanent.	*Every warranty must eventually expire.*
Desires lead only to more desires.	*Who owns a compact disc player must purchase compact discs.*
Laziness is an obstacle to perfection.	*Vacation leads to poor quality control.*
Ignorance results in endless rounds of death and rebirth.	*Attend top university or face eternal shame.*
Poverty leads to anger and hatred.	*A homogeneous middle-class society is a peaceful one.*
Avoid all worldly distractions.	*Ignore the suffering of non-Japanese people.*
Help others find the path to joy.	*Sell high-quality products to every person on Earth.*

ROAD SIGNS

I f you must drive in Japan, be sure to familiarize
yourself with the unique local roadsigns.

WHITE RICE
NEXT 900 KM

SLOW
WRESTLERS

GIVE IT UP FOR
KABUKI AHEAD

MINIATURE CITY
NEXT LEFT

LIFE IS LIKE A RIVER,
NEXT 10 KM

THE CROWDED SUBWAY, JUDO AND YOU

Japanese subways are fast, efficient and convenient. They can also be extraordinarily crowded. White-gloved "pushers" will kindly shove you into a rush-hour train.

Japanese *en route* can be extremely rude. They have a saying: "*Tabi no haji wa kakisute,*" or "The traveler's shame can be brushed off." New York subways seem almost genteel compared to those in Japan.

Men shove old ladies aside for seats, and you're sure to be knocked around by people heading for the door. Women may find unwelcome body parts pressed against them. A few phrases, combined with proper judo strikes, may help you vent some of your frustration.

INSULT	JUDO RESPONSE	VERBAL ASSAULT	JAPANESE
Reading paper in your face.	Silent meditation: "May Death Come Soon to Infidels."	None	
Falling fast asleep, using you as mattress.	Wet willie-san (moistened finger poked into enemy ear).	"Good morning!"	おはよう！ **Ohayo!** *Oh-HI-oh!*
Strong shove.	Grab opponent's suit coat side pocket. Rip downwards, firmly.	"So sorry."	ゴメンナサイ。 **Gomennasai.** *Go-MEN-nah-SIGH.*
Lascivious rubbing.	Strike firmly at tender organs.	"Police! Arrest this pervert!"	おまわりさん！ 痴漢を つかまえて！ **Omawarisan! Chikan o tsukamaete!** *Oh-MAH-wah-ree-san! Chee-KAN oh TSKA-mah-teh!*

ZEN CAB: WHAT IS FINAL DESTINATION OF MOTIONLESS TAXI?

Like almost everything else in Japan, taxis are new, expensive and spotless. The fares are so high that you half-expect the drivers to speak a little English and serve drinks.

They may wear white gloves, but *untenshusan* won't speak your language. They can't read your mind, either. Explaining where you want to go is complicated by the fact that few streets have names and building numbers are chosen according to the whims of several especially cruel Shinto gods.

Ask your host or concierge to write directions to your destination on a slip of paper for your driver, and carry several thousand yen—in cash—for your fare.

| **This is where I am going.** | Koko e itte kudasai. | ここへ 行って下さい。 | *KOH-koh eh EE-tay koo-dah-SIGH.* |

Could we be there in two hours?	Ni-jikan de tsukimasuka?	2時間で 着きますか？	*Nee-jee-KAHN day tsoo-KEE-mah-SKA?*
In time for the next vernal equinox, then?	Rainen no shunbun madeniwa tsukima-suyone?	来年の春分 までには 着きますよね？	*RYE-nen no SHUN-bun mah-day-NEE-wa TSOO-kee-mah-soo-YOH-nay?*
Say, this is an impressive traffic jam!	Nante komikata nandesho!	なんて混み方 なんでしょ！	*NON-tay koh-mee-KAH-tah nan-DAY-sho!*
We haven't moved a millimeter in half an hour.	San-ju punkan ichi-miri mo susunde inai.	30分間 1ミリも進んで いない。	*SAHN-joo poon-kan EE-chee-MEE-ree mo soo-SUN-day ee-NIGH.*
Sir, I think you are too polite.	Moshi moshi, anata wa hikaeme sugimasenka.	もしもし、 あなたは控え目 すぎませんか。	*Moosh moosh, ah-NAH-tah wa HEE-ka-AY-may soo-gee-ma-SEN-ka.*
Do you mind if I honk?	Watashi ni kurakushon osasete morae-masuka?	私に クラクション 押させて もらえますか？	*Wah-TAH-shee nee koo-RAK-shon OH-sah-SAY-tay MOH-rah-ay-MOSS-ka?*

EMERGENCIES

Disorder is rare in Japan, but in case of emergency, dialing 110 will reach the police and 119 an ambulance or fire crew. You will need a couple of key phrases.

Emergency!	Tasukete oisogi!	たすけて、大急ぎ！	Tah-soo-KAY-tay OH-ee-SOH-ghee!
I am at the corner of two nameless streets!	Nanashi no nihon no michi no kado ni imasu!	名無しの二本の道の角にいます！	NAH-nah-SHEE no NEE-hone no MEE-chee no KAH-doh nee ee-MOSS!
I am near a sushi bar/ electronics store/ boutique!	Sushiya/ denkiya/ buttiku no soba desu!	寿司屋／電器屋／ブティックのそばです！	Soo-SHEE-ah/ den-KEE-ya/ boo-tee-koo no so-ba DAY-soo!
I need an ambulance/ fire truck/ policeman/ large cash advance!	Kyukyusha/ shobosha omawarisan/ tairyo no genkin no maegari ga imasugu hitsuyo nanda!	救急車／消防車／おまわりさん／大量の現金の前借りが今すぐ必要なんだ！	Kee-yoo-kee-yoo-sha/SHO-bo-sha/oh-MA-wa-ree-san/ TIE-ree-oh no GHEN-keen no ma-AY-ga-ree ga ee-ma-SOO-goo HEET-soo-YOH NON-dah!

PLAY-BY-PLAY SUMO

Sumo (pronounced "smo"), fat-power wrestling, is over a thousand years old. Wrestlers stomp their feet, clap their hands, throw salt and lift their fat eyelids to glare at each other.

A little knowledgeable commentary will give you more prestige in the eyes of your hosts.

What a mighty mountain of meat!	Nante okina niku no katamari desho!	なんて大きな 肉のかたまり でしょう！	*NON-tay OH-keen-ah NEE-koo no KA-ta-MA-ree day-SHO!*
He looks as grand and immobile as Mount Fuji.	Okikute ugokasenai fuji-san mitai da.	大きくて 動かせない 富士山みたいだ。	*Oh-KEE-koo-tay OO-go-ka-SEN-ai FOO-ji-san mee-TAI da.*
Whoops! He isn't as imposing flat on his back, is he!	Are! Taoreteruto sonnani osoroshikumo naina?	あれ！ 倒れていると そんなにも 恐ろしくも ないなあ？	*Ah-RAY! TAH-ray-tay-ROO-toh so-NAH-nee oh-so-ROSH-koo-mo na-ee-NAH?*

BARBARIC BASEBALL CHEERS

Corporate life is so pervasive that even *beisu-boru* teams represent giant corporations, not cities or regions. And whether they're on the job or at a ball game, the Japanese are comfortable taking orders and preserving harmony.

Fans, even the most rabid, usually remain silent and motionless until professional cheerleaders tell them to make a team cheer or sing a team song. Amaze fans and players by being the only person among thousands to yell insults at the top of your lungs.

Hey batter batter!	Ohi batta batta!	オーイ、バッターバッター！	*OH-ee bah-TAH bah-TAH!*
Stand up, little fellow!	Chikkoino, okiagareyo!	ちっこいの、起きあがれよ！	*CHEE-koh EE-noh, oh-KEE-ah-gah-RAY-oh!*
Easy out! Easy out!	Kantan! Kantan!	かんたん！かんたん！	*Kahn-TAHN! Kahn-TAHN!*
Aw! My mother has a better swing!	Ah, uchi no kachan no ho ga ee battingu suruyo!	アー、うちの母ちゃんの方がいいバッティングするよ！	*Ah, OO-chee no KAH-chan no ho ga ay bah-TEEN-goo soo-roo-yo!*

ENTERTAINMENT AND OBSESSION

Where's your makeup, you geisha!	Okesho wa doshitano, geisha-san!	お化粧は どうしたの、 芸者さん！	*Oh-KESH-oh wa DOSH-tah-no GAY-sha-sahn!*
Shame! Public humiliation!	Ahoka! Sodai gomi!	あほか！ 粗大ゴミ！	*Ah-ho-ka! SO-dai go-mee!*
Forget baseball!	Yakyu, yame chimae!	野球 やめちまえ！	*YAK-ee-yoo, YAH-may chee-MAI!*
Go get us some tea!	Ocha kunde koi!	お茶 くんでこい！	*Oh-CHA kund-eh-KOY!*

AUTHENTIC BASEBALL CHEERS

**O fighting spirit! Fly, fireball, into the sky!
O Giants with honorable diamond playing strong!
Giants! Giants! Go! Go! Heroes!**

**Storm clouds penetrated! By balls to the star of
   victory!
O Giants with honorable name—tomorrow!
Grow! Our team! Brave and heroic!
Giants! Giants! Go! Go! Heroes!**

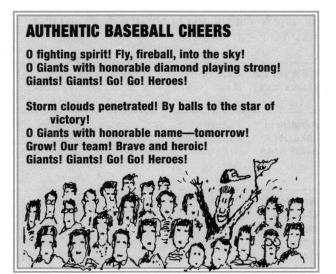

GOLF AS WAR

Membership in a top Japanese country club can cost over a million dollars. Serious golfers are therefore every bit as elite today as the samurai were in feudal times.

Like sword-fighting, *gorufu* suits the Japanese taste for Zen—the harder one tries, the worse one plays. The Japanese also like activities that require special clothes. They purchase extravagant golf wardrobes and look extremely silly.

If you are invited to play a round in Japan, never fear. Your opponents may adopt samurai spirit and attempt to cut you to ribbons, but they can't play worth spit.

What are the stakes here?	Kakekin wa ikura desuka?	かけ金は いくらですか？	*KAH-kay-kin wa ee-koo-rah DESK-ah?*
A bottle of sake per hole? Done.	Pahoru goto osake ippon? Kekko desu ne.	パーホールごと、 お酒1本？ 結構ですね。	*Pa-HO-roo GO-toh oh-SAH-kay ee-PON? KEK-oh DAY-soo nay.*
Well done! That was a long drive for a man your size.	Yatta! Karada no wari ni yoku tobi mashita ne.	やった！ 体の割によく 飛びましたね。	*Ya-TAH! Kah-RA-da no WAH-ree nee YOH-koo TOH-bee MOSH-tah nay*

ENTERTAINMENT AND OBSESSION

Ah! Bad luck, Suzuki-san!	Ah, un ga warui ne, suzuki-san!	アー、運が悪いね、鈴木さん！	*Ah, uhn ga wah-ROO-ee-nay, soo-ZOO-kee-san!*
Only a meter short of the green!	Gurin ni ichi metoru tarinai!	グリーンに1メートル足りてない！	*Goo-REEN nee EE-chee MAY-toh-roo TAH-ree-nigh!*
And such a deep bunker, too.	Soreni nante hidoi banka nan desho.	それに何てひどいバンカーなんでしょ。	*Soh-REN-ee NON-tay hee-DOY bahn-KA non DAY-sho.*
You'll need a ladder to get down into that one.	Oriru noni hashigo ga iru to omoimasu.	おりるのにハシゴがいると思います。	*Oh-REE-roo NOH-nee ha-SHEE-go ga EE-roo toh oh-MO-ee-MOSS.*
Would you like to borrow my excellent sand wedge?	Watashi no jotona sandowejji o okashi shimashoka?	私の上等なサンドウェッジをお貸ししましょうか？	*Wah-TAH-shee no jo-TOH-nah SAN-doh-WEH-jee oh oh-KOSH-ee SHEE-ma-SHOH-ka?*

DEFENSIVE DRIVING

Gorufu is so popular that some people practice for years without getting onto a course. They will swing umbrellas, rolled-up newspapers and "air clubs," anything to display their good taste.

The closest they may get to actual golf is at multistory driving ranges. If you'd like to hit balls at a Japanese range, you'll need a few phrases.

A big bucket of balls, please.	Okina baketsu ippai no boru, onegai shimasu.	大きなバケツ 1杯のボール、 お願いします。	*OH-key-nah bah-KET-soo ee-PIE no bo-roo, oh-nay-GUY shee MOSS.*
Do you have anything near the ground floor?	Jimen ni chikai tokoro arimasuka?	地面に近い ところ ありますか？	*JEE-men nee chee-KAI toh-KOH-roh ah-ree-MOSS-kah?*
I'm looking for a sense of realism.	Jissaidori ni yaritain desu.	実際通りに やりたいんです。	*Jee-SAI-doh-ree nee yar-ee-TINE DAY-soo.*
Do you also rent helmets?	Herumetto mo arimasuka?	ヘルメットも ありますか？	*Hay-roo-MAY-toh mo AR-ee-MOSS-ka?*
The other golfers look a little wild tonight.	Konya wa minna aretemasune.	今夜はみんな 荒れてますね。	*KOH-nee-ah wa MEE-nah ah-RAY-tay-MOSS-nay.*

CEREMONY OF THE BON BON

Those who violate the stark rules of gift-giving may be tattooed as boors forever. To achieve the rank of Gift Master you must follow these rules:

Wait for them to give. If you present your hosts with chocolate and they have none for you, your bonbons will be received as small brown insults. By tradition, the recipients will be compelled to destroy you.

Don't be cheap or extravagant. A briefcase full of unmarked bills is as embarrassing as a Budweiser T-shirt. The recipient is likely to respond with a series of firm kicks to your head and midriff.

Do not give gifts in multiples of four. The number four means death to the Japanese. An equivalent gift in the United States is a dead fish.

Wrap carefully in Japanese rice paper, the most important part of the gift. Content is less important than form. As you reach the level of Gift Master, your need to give and receive actual gifts will gradually disappear. A hollow box of rice paper will be enough.

THE PRACTICAL GAIJIN

STRAW BED & RAW BREAKFAST

Travelers can get a taste of traditional Japan by staying in a *ryokan* (guest house).

If you are successful in obtaining a reservation, remove your shoes upon entering the hotel. Your maid will lead you to your room; do not step on the tatami mats. Guests take communal baths before dinner is served in their rooms.

What pleasant furnishings!	**Nante suteki na oheya desho!**	なんて すてきなお部屋 でしょう！	*NON-tay STEK-ee na oh-HAY-ah day-SHO!*
A table and two cushions!	**Teiburu to nimai no zabuton!**	テーブルと 二枚の ざぶとん！	*TAY-boo-roo toh NEE-mai no ZAH-boo-TOHN!*
Hey, who needs a chair/sofa/ bed/TV anyway?	**Choto, isu/ sofa/beddo/ terebi nante iranaiyone?**	ちょっと、 イス／ソファ／ ベッド／テレビ なんていら ないよね？	*CHOH-toh, EE-soo/so-FA/ BED-oh/tay-RAY-bee NON-tay ee-rah-NAI-oh-neh?*

THE PRACTICAL GAIJIN

Madam, please change the sheet on my futon.	Okami san, futon no shitsu o kaete kudasai.	おかみさん、フトンのシーツをかえて下さい。	*Oh-KAH-me sahn, FOO-ton no SHEET-soo oh ka-AY-tay koo-dah-SIGH.*
It smells of pickled eel.	Unagi no tsukemono mitaina nioi da.	うなぎの漬物みたいな匂いだ。	*Oo-NAH-ghee no TSOO-kay-moh-noh MEE-tah-EE-nah nee-OH-ee da.*
One more thing—would you bring me toast and coffee for breakfast?	Eto sorekara —tosuto to kohi no choshoku arimasuka.	エート、それから…。トーストとコーヒーの朝食ありますか。	*AY-toh so-RAY-ka-RA— TOAST-oh toh KOH-HEE no CHOASH-koo AR-ee-MOSS-kah.*
No rice. No fish. No raw egg. Please.	No gohan. No sushi. No nama tamago. Onegai shimasu.	ノーごはん、ノーすし、ノー生卵、お願いします。	*No go-HAHN. No SOO-shee. No NAH-ma tah-MA-go. OH-nay-GUY shee-MOSS.*
I am too barbaric to eat a Japanese breakfast.	Nihonshoku o tabetsukete inai yabanjin desu.	日本食を食べつけていない野蛮人です。	*NEE-hone-SHO-koo oh TAH-bay-soo-KAY-tay ee-NAI YA-bon-JEEN DAY-soo.*

WISE LOSS OF FACE

Some Japanese bars take advantage of cultural taboos by not listing prices; men consider it shameful to ask about price before ordering. This can be hazardous for those not flying on company plastic—a couple of rounds of drinks may cost hundreds of dollars. Some establishments, known as *boryoku* (violence bars), employ karate experts to extract payment from balky customers.

If you do ask about prices, try to do so privately, as your Japanese guests will be ashamed by your queries and will never go out with you again.

How much is whiskey/beer/ sake?	Uisuki/biru/ sake wa ikura desuka?	ウイスキー／ ビール／酒は いくらですか？	*OO-ee-soo-KEE/BEE-roo/SAH-kay wah ee-koo-rah DESK-ah?*
Thirty dollars each?	Ippai, yonsen gohyaku en?	1杯、 四千五百円？	*Ee-PAI, YON-sen GO-hee-AH-koo en?*
What do we get with our drinks?	Ippai ni tsuki nani ga tsuite kuruno?	1杯につき何が ついてくるの？	*Ee-PAI nee TSOO-key NAH-nee ga TSO-ee-tay koo-loo-noh?*

Polar ice and silk napkins?	Nankyoku no kori to kinu no napukin demo kuruno?	南極の氷と絹のナプキンでもくるの？	*NANK-oh-koo no KOH-ree toh KEE-noo no NAP-oo-kin DAY-mo KOO-roo-no?*
And a little respect from a bartender?	Batensan no okini sawari mashitaka?	バーテンさんのお気にさわりましたか？	*BAH-ten-sahn no oh-KEE-nee sah-WAH-ree MOSH-tock-ah?*

RENT-A-COFFIN

Kapuseru hoteru (capsule hotels) were designed for two sorts of customers: men who miss their trains and vampires on tight budgets. "Rooms" are divided into large coffins, stacked three high and made of plastic for easy cleaning. *Totemo benri!* (How convenient!) Naturally, each coffin is equipped with a mattress and TV.

Kapuseru hoteru can be found near almost any large train station, but they are not recommended for people of normal size. If you are forced to stay in one, remember, don't wear shoes in your windowless plastic cubbyhole! That would be uncivilized!

VISITING THE JAPANESE HOME

The Japanese entertain at home about as often as we entertain in our closets, but if you do visit a private home, be ready with a few compliments.

Your garden is like a jewel.	Hoseki no yona niwa desune.	宝石のような庭ですね。	*HO-sek-ee no yo-nah NEE-wa DAY-soo-nay.*
As the breeze flows through the shrub, my heart is at peace.	Midori o nukeru soyokaze ga, watashi no kokoro o nagomasete kure masu.	緑をぬけるそよ風が、私の心をなごませてくれます。	*Mee-DOH-ree oh noo-KAY-roo SOY-oh-KAW-zay gah, wa-TAH-shee no koh-KOH-roh oh NAH-go-MAH-say-tay KOO-ray moss.*
The stone in the pond is as fluid and elegant as a mythical bird.	Ike no ishi wa shinwa no tori no yoni yuga de furyu desu.	池の石は神話の鳥のように優雅で風流です。	*EE-kay no EE-shee wa SHEEN-wa no TOH-ree no YOH-nee YOO-ga day FOOR-yoo DAY-soo.*
And in the living room, I am struck by the Hello Kitty motif.	Ima no kitty-chan no kazaritsuke niwa kando shimashita.	居間のキティちゃんの飾りつけには感動しました。	*EE-ma no KEE-tee-chan no ka-zah-REET-soo-kay NEE-wa kan-DOH shee-MOSH-tah.*

DINING ETIQUETTE FOR BARBARIANS

While Japan has one of the most formal cultures ever invented, some of its customs make perfect sense. We all know that shoes are dirty things, for example; in Japan they are removed before entering a home or *zashiki* (a private room in a restaurant). On a trip to the *toile*, you must change into special rubber slippers. Failure to do so will win you the social standing of a sewer rat.

When using chopsticks **never**:

- Use them to pass food to someone else. This is how the bones of dead family members are handled by Buddhist priests;

- Stick them vertically into the rice. This turns the meal into an offering for the dead;

- Lick them unless you want to take your fellow diners to bed;

- Display your grasp of Zen by trying to catch flies with your chopsticks. It's much harder than it looks.

HONORABLE TEA

Coffee (*kohi*) is becoming more popular, but honorable tea (*o-cha*) remains as essential to Japanese life as rice and microchips. In offices and homes, tea is served at ten o'clock in the morning and again at three in the afternoon.

The ideal green tea is clear, bitter and still boiling when it hits the roof of your mouth. It is potent: one cup is usually enough to get an unconscious reveler out of the gutter and on his way to work with a smile on his face and a pulse of 160.

Honorable tea? Yes, please!	Ocha? Hai, onegai shimasu.	お茶？はい、お願いします！	*Oh-CHA? Hai, OH-nay-GUY shee-MOSS.*
I drank some after I got off the plane last week.	Senshu hikoki kara orite ippai nomimashita.	先週、飛行機から降りて1杯飲みました。	*San-SHOO hee-KOH-kee KA-rah oh-REE-tay ee-PAI noh-min-MOSH-tah.*
I haven't slept since.	Sore irai neteimasen.	それ以来寝ていません。	*So-ray ee-RAI nay-TAY-ee-MOSS-en.*
I have many evil thoughts.	Osoroshii kangae nimo osoware masu.	恐ろしい考えにも襲われます。	*OH-so-ROH-shee kahn-GAY NEE-moh OH-so-WA-ray MOSS.*

In short, I love green tea.	Demo kekkyoku, watashi wa ocha ga sukidesu.	でも結局、私はお茶が好きです。	*DAY-moh cake-YOH-koo, wa-TOSH-ee wa oh-CHA ga soo-key-DAY-soo.*
Do you know where I could find a nickel bag of the stuff?	Nikkeru-bag wa dokode teni hairi masuka?	ニッケルバックは、どこで手に入りますか？	*NEE-kay-roo-bag wah DOH-koh-DAY ten-EE ha-EE-ree MOSS-ka?*

SAKE TO ME

Sake is not just a drink: it is a holy sacrament of conversation, meditation and oblivion. Thus there are special rules regarding its use.

Don't let anyone's sake cup become empty. And don't drink the last few drops from your cup; wait until it is refilled.

When sake is poured, take a sip immediately. It will be boiling hot, but you must not lose face. You can seek medical attention later.

As your vision and speech begin to blur, try not to throw up or ridicule anyone's haircut. Shots of hot tea may revive you enough to keep drinking.

AVOIDING AMBULATORY FOOD

There are two things to watch out for in Japanese restaurants: prices and food. If prices aren't marked on the menu, beware—your meal may cost more than a piece of Tokyo real estate. The food, meanwhile, will be anxious and upset—keep fingers, hair, and clothing away from the animals on the the the table.

That looks good.	Yosasou desune.	良さそうですね。	*YO-sah-so dess-NAY.*
Please tie it down/cook it.	Osaete kudasai/ryori shite.	おさえて下さい／料理して。	*OH-sah-ay-TAY koo-DA-sai ree-OH-ree shee-TAY.*
The broth is for drowning?	Kono dashijiru de oboresaseru no desuka?	このダシ汁でおぼれさせるのですか？	*Koh-NOH DAH-shee-JEE-roo day OH-boh-RAY-sah-SAY-roo no DESK-ah?*
How the honorable shrimp struggle as they choke to death!	Ebi no idaina saigo desu!	エビの偉大な最期です！	*Eh-BEE no ee-DAI-nah sai-GO DAY-soo!*

Do you serve any completely dead domestic animals?	Ugoki dasanai kachiku no niku, arimasenka?	動き出さない家畜の肉、ありませんか？	*Oo-GO-kee DA-sah-NAI KA-chee-KOO noh nee-KOO, ah-REE-mah-SEN-KA?*
How about some fried/ boiled beef?	Sukiyaki/ shabu-shabu wa arimasuka?	すきやき／シャブシャブはありますか？	*Skee-YA-kee shah-BOO-shah-BOO wa AH-ree-MOSS-ka?*
Great. Bring me some ketchup/Coke with that, please.	Yokatta. Kechappu/ kora mo kudasai.	よかった。ケチャップ／コーラも下さい。	*Yoh-KAH-TAH. KAY-chah-poo/ koh-rah mo KOO-DA-sai.*

FUGU ROULETTE

Fugu is blowfish, prepared by highly-trained chefs who remove most—but not all—of the fish's deadly poison. Chefs do make mistakes, of course, but that's what makes fugu so exciting.

No, please. After you.	Iie, dozo. Osakini.	いいえ。どうぞお先に。	*EE-ay, DOH-zoh, OH-sah-KEE-nee.*
I hate to disturb the artwork of the chef.	Shefu no geijutsu sakuhin o kowashitaku nai.	シェフの芸術作品をこわしたくない。	*SHEF-oo no guy-JOOT-soo SAK-oo-HEEN oh koh-WAH-shee-TOK nai.*
Well, how is it?	Sate, Dodesuka?	さて、どうですか？	*SAH-tay, DOH-desk?*
You look okay.	Daijobusou desune.	大丈夫そうですね。	*Dai-JO-boo-soo dess-NAY.*
What the hell, I'll have some.	Konattara, watashi mo itadakimasho.	こうなったら、私もいただきましょう。	*KOH-nah-tah-rah, wah-TOSH mo ee-TAH-dah-kee-imosh-OH.*
Hey, you're eating my share!	Chotto, watashi no bun mo tabeteru!	ちょっと私の分も食べてる！	*CHO-toh, wah-TOSH no boon moh TAH-bay-TAY-roo!*

SLURP AS BUDDHA

Like each stone in a pond, each slurp in a meal represents a chance to touch perfection. But different slurps are required for different dishes, just as each stone has its own place.

Soup is slurped gently but firmly. Eyes are directed skyward, not to the bowl, as this would make the diner appear cross-eyed. This soup-slurp is known as "Praying Mantis Style."

The long noodle is slurped without regard for launched vegetables or flung broth. The steady flowing motion, much like the smooth tongue-flicking of a small aardvark in the autumn moonlight, inspires the name, "Esteemed Ant-Eater Method."

The slice of boiled pork is slurped while offering silent thanks to the spirit of the departed pig for its contribution to the meal. The master diner simply pokes his or her face into the bowl. Once the pork is grasped, the head is thrown back and the slice inhaled so quickly that the motion is invisible to the Western eye. This is known as the "Wild-Dog-in-the-Alley Technique."

IMPRESSING YOUR GEISHA

You're not likely to meet any authentic geisha, but you probably will meet their less-well-trained counterparts known as *hosutesu*. Geisha and *hosutesu* are not prostitutes. They pride themselves on their refined charm and culture, so ambitious men do well to adopt a little of their own.

I am honored to meet you, miss.	Oaidekite koeidesu, ojosama.	お会いできて光栄です、お嬢様。	*OH-ai-DAY-kee-tay KOH-ai-DAY-soo, oh-JOH-sah-ma.*
You are as beautiful as spring's first cherry blossom.	Anata wa haru ichiban no sakura no yoni utsukushii.	あなたは春一番の桜の様に美しい。	*Ah-NAH-ta wa HA-roo EE-chee-bahn no sa-KOO-ra no YOH-nee OOTS-koo-shee.*
Read any good haiku lately?	Haiku demo hitotsu dodesuka?	俳句でも一つどうですか？	*HAI-koo DAY-mo hee-TOTE-soo doh-DESK-ah?*
Which poet is your favorite?	Dare ga suki desuka?	誰が好きですか？	*DAH-ray ga soo-kee DESK-ah?*
You recite wonderfully.	Nante subarashii okoe desho.	なんてすばらしい御声でしょう。	*NON-tay soo-ba-ROSH oh-KOH-ay day-SHO.*

But haiku is such a short form.	Haiku wa mijikai desune.	俳句は 短いですね。	*HAI-koo wa MEE-jee-kai dess-NAY.*
I happen to have an epic poem with me.	Subarashii shio motte kite imasu.	すばらしい 詩を持って きています。	*Soo-ba-ROSH SHEE-oh MO-tay KEE-tay ee-MOSS.*
Come back to my hotel and let me show it to you.	Hoteru ni itte issho ni yomi masenka.	ホテルに 行って一緒に 読みませんか。	*Ho-TAY-roo nee EE-tay EE-sho nee YOH-mee ma-SEN-kah.*

GETTING NAKED IN JAPAN

A s high-tech as Japan may seem, millions of Japanese homes have no plumbing. Many people go to *ofuroya* (public baths) to bathe and relax in communal tubs.

Everyone washes at basins before getting into the tubs. For filthy *gaijin*, this is especially important because bathwater is reused and regulars may be disgusted to share it with you. You can take advantage of their disgust, however, to get a whole tub to yourself.

Pardon me, but have you a bigger towel?	Sumimasen, okina taoru arimasuka?	すみません、大きなタオルありますか？	*SOO-mee-MA-sen, oh-KEE-nah tay-OH-roo AH-ree-MOSS-ka?*
I don't want to frighten anyone.	Hokanohito o odokashi taku nai.	他の人をおどかしたくない。	*Ho-KA-no-HEE-toh oh OH-doh-KA-shee TA-koo nai.*
Good evening. Is there room for me in this tub?	Konbanwa. Watashi no hairu tokoro arimasuka?	今晩は。私の入るところありますか？	*Kon-BAHN-wa. Wa-TA-shee no HI-roo toh-KOH-roh AH-ree-MOSS-ka?*
Ayee! Hot as molten lava!	Atsui! Yogan mitai!	熱い！溶岩みたい！	*Aht-soo-ee! Yo-GAHN mee-TAI!*

I like you.	Anata ga sukidesu.	あなたが 好きです。	*Ah-NAH-tah ga SOO-key-DESS.*
Do you mind if I sit in your lap?	Anata no hiza ni suwattemo yoroshii deshoka?	あなたの ヒザに坐っても よろしいで しょうか？	*Ah-NAH-tah no HEE-za nee SOO-wa-TAY-mo yo-ROH-shee day-SHOKE?*
Please massage my thighs.	Watashi no huto momo o monde kudasai.	私の太モモを もんで下さい。	*Wah-TOSH no HOO-toh MOH-moh oh MONE-day KOO-dah-SIGH.*
Hey! Where's everybody going?	Are! Minna doko ittano?	あれ！みんな どこ行ったの？	*Ah-RAY! MEEN-ah DOH-ko ee-TAH-noh?*

THE KARAOKE BAR

B usiness associates go out in a group nearly every night. So profound is their boredom and so heavy is their drinking that they entertain each other by singing popular songs accompanied by taped music.

The Japanese enjoy "Love Me Tender" and "Home on the Range," but if you really want to make friends and influence people, serenade them with "Kimigayo."

May thy glorious, glorious reign Last for ages, myriad ages, Till the tiny pebbles small Into mighty rocks shall grow— Hoary moss shall over- grow them all.	Kimi ga yo wa Chiyo ni yachiyo ni Sazare ishi no Iwao to narite—Koke no musu made.	君が代は 千代に八千代に 小石の巌と なりて苔の むすまで	*KEE-mee ga yo wa CHEE-oh nee ya-CHEE- oh nee Sa-ZA- ray EE-shee no Ee-WAY-oh toh na-REE-tay— Ko-kay no MOO-soo MA-day*

ALE BONDING

The Japanese tradition of fellowship with *nakama* (business buddies) is called *otsukiai*. Drinking too much and acting like dirty little boys is a tradition among company men.

If you'd like to gain the trust of your associates, you must get so staggering drunk that you'll willingly pick up a microphone and serenade a barful of giggling men.

Cheers!	**Kampai!**	かんぱーい。	*Kam-PAI!*
Chug it!	**Ikki, ikki!**	一気、一気!	*Icky, icky!*
Bring us a whole bottle!	**Botoru ippon motte kite!**	ボトル1本 もってきて!	*Boh-TOH-roo ee-PON MOH-tay KEE-tay!*
Hey Kazuko-san, you look a little green!	**Chotto kazukosan, aozameter-uyo!**	ちょっと かず子さん 青ざめてるよ!	*CHOH-toh ka-ZOO-ko-san, ay-oh-ZA-may-tay-ROO-yoh!*
Get him a drink/ wheelchair/ doctor!	**Hayaku nomimono/ kurumaisu/ isha o kare ni!**	はやく、 飲物／車イス／ 医者を彼に!	*Hah-YA-koo NO-mee-MO-no/koo-roo-MY-soo/EESH-ah oh KA-ray nee!*
Hey, this is fun!	**Koitsua omoshiroiya!**	こいつあ、 おもしろいや!	*Ko-eet-soo-ah OH-mo-shee-ROY-ah!*

"LIFE" IN A JAPANESE FIRM

To work for a Japanese company you must forget your Western ways. You will be expected to dedicate your body and soul to work. Nothing can take precedence over the needs of the corporation, including your own emotional or financial well-being. And the firm has no room for stars, mavericks or non-Japanese executives, no matter what their talents.

The following phrases will help you in job interviews. You may also use them as mantras in your effort to hypnotize yourself into wanting to work for a Japanese firm.

I want to sing the company song six mornings a week for the rest of my life.	Shinumade, shu ni muika, maiasa shaka o utaitai to omoimasu.	死ぬまで、週に6日、毎朝社歌を唄いたいと思います。	*SHEE-noo-MAH-day, shoo nee moo-EE-ka, my-AH-sah SHA-ka OO-tai-tai toh oh-MO-ee-MAH-soo.*
I will always agree with my superiors, even when they are totally wrong.	Tatoe karera ga machigatte itemo, watashi no joshi niwa sakarai masen.	たとえ彼らがまちがっていても、私の上司には逆らえません。	*Ta-TOH ka-RAY-rah ga MAH-chee-GA-tay ee-TAY-mo, wa-TASH no JO-shee NEE-wa SA-ka-RAI MOSS-en.*

WORKING FOR THE JAPANESE

I do not care about making money.	Okanemoke ni kyomi wa arimasen.	お金儲けに興味は有りません。	*Oh-KAH-nay-MO-kay nee kee-YOH-mee wa AH-ree-MOSS-en.*
My dream is to be a tiny cog in a huge and honorable machine.	Yumei na daigaisha no hitotsu no haguruma ni naritai.	有名な大会社の一つの歯車になりたい。	*YOO-may na dai-GAI-shah no hee-TOTE-soo no ha-GOO-roo-ma nee NA-ree-TAI.*
When my firm has no more use for me, I will go quietly to my death.	Watashi ni yo ga nakunattara, sumiyakani hakabe e mairimasu.	私に用がなくなったら、すみやかに墓場へまいります。	*Wa-TAH-shee nee yo ga nah-KOO-nah-tah-rah, SOO-mee-ah-KAH-nee ha-KAH-ba ay MAR-ee-MOSS.*

COMPANY SONGS

The company song is an important part of corporate indoctrination in Japan. The following is a typical example. In order to remain happy in your job, insert the name of your firm in the song of your choice and sing it at least twice a day.

O GLORIOUS CORPORATION! IDAI NA KAISHA!			
We find meaning of life at (company name)!	Jinsei no ikigai o (kaisha mei) de mitsuketa!	人生の 生きがいを （社名）で 見つけた！	*JIN-say no EE-kee-GAI oh (company name) day MEET-skay-tah!*
Real family is here in enormous office building!	Kyodai biru no naka wa mina kazoku!	巨大ビルの 内は皆家族！	*Kai-oh-DAI BEE-roo no NAH-ka wa MEE-na KAZ-koo!*
We love our unity!	Icchi danketsu shiyo!	一致 団結しよう！	*EE-chee dahn-KET-soo shee-YO!*
Ten thousand employees pressed tightly together.	Ichi-mannin no nakama no katai kessoku.	1万人の仲間の 固い結束。	*EE-chee MA-nin-no nah-KA-mah no ka-TAI KESS-koo.*

WORKING FOR THE JAPANESE

We find joy and harmony around the clock!	Tokei no ugoki ni yorokobi to chowa ga kizamareru!	時計の動きに喜びと調和が刻まれる！	*Toh-KAY no WOO-go-kee nee yo-roh-KOH-bee toh CHO-wa ga KEE-za-ma-RAY-roo!*
We never contradict our superiors!	Uwayaku to shototsu shinai!	上役と衝突しない！	*OO-wa-YA-koo toh SHOTE-tsoo shee-NAI!*
Happiness for all people as company grows ever larger.	Kaisha no hatten wa jibun no seicho da.	会社の発展は自分の成長だ。	*KAI-sha no HA-ten wa jee-BUN no SAY-cho da.*
And finally swallows entire planet!	Chikyu o nomikomo!	地球をのみこもう！	*Cheek-yoo oh no-MEE-ko-MO!*

BOW TO CONQUER

The Japanese expect handshakes from *gaijin*. To them we are barbarians who could never grasp the excruciating subtleties of the bow. Attempts at bowing are appreciated, however, and can do much to ingratiate you with the natives.

A proper bow is crisp and made from the waist—it is not a nod. Hold your arms stiffly at your sides, as if you were offering to have your head chopped off. In close quarters, bow at an angle to avoid knocking your opponent unconscious.

Pause slightly at the bottom of your bow, both to show respect and to examine the quality of your counterpart's footwear. Rank is not always obvious, but you should assume that people wearing shoes more expensive and well-polished than your own outrank you. Bow longer and more deeply to them.

But whatever you do, don't take the bowing too seriously. The Japanese study it their whole lives; you cannot ever hope to become totally proficient. Mastering the mechanical details is difficult and adopting the proper attitude is close to impossible.

FLIGHT OF THE CRANE AND THE PROPER INTRODUCTION

In Japan, a man is his work. A *meishi* (business card) therefore sums up a person's identity and value as a human being; treat it with respect.

Your own card should be printed in English on one side and Japanese on the other. (Your hotel can print proper cards in 24 hours.) Upon introduction, pull a card from its special case in a single smooth motion without excessive flourish, much as the crane takes wing on a winter morning. Bow as you exchange cards, holding yours in such a way that the recipient can read it.

If he draws his sword, run.

STARTING A BUSINESS IN JAPAN

The world's second-largest market has some of the most homogenous consumers. In other words, if you can sell your product to 200 Japanese, you can probably sell it to 20 million. But before you start counting your yen, consider two barriers. The bureaucracy, number one, would make the Dalai Lama tear his hair out, if he had any, and swim for home. The system seems designed to stifle foreign businesses and products in Japan. The other barrier is an army of industry groups that would make a Sicilian mob boss blush.

At the core of each gang, called a *keiretsu*, you'll find a large bank and a trading company. Its octopus arms include firms in energy, transportation, manufacturing, insurance, retail and so on. They work together, and if you threaten any of them, you may find them all arrayed against you.

Oddly enough, financial difficulties have not made Japan more open to competition, and few Japanese consumers object to the gangs' big markups. The best approach may be to find Japanese partners and make sure they keep their hands where you can see them.

TRANSLATING ATTITUDES

Japanese business decisions are based on trust and long-term relationships, not on price or quality. To win that trust, you have to play the game their way.

Many of the qualities we value in our salespeople are disastrous in Japan, so you must learn how attitudes translate between cultures.

WESTERN ATTITUDE	JAPANESE TRANSLATION
Confident	*Boastful*
Direct	*Crude*
Open	*Foolish*
Forceful	*Pushy*
Eager	*Weak*
Anxious	*Defeated*

JAPANESE ATTITUDE	WESTERN TRANSLATION
Powerful	*Inert*
Strong	*Intransigent*
Patient	*Catatonic*
Harmonious	*Soul-less*
Superior	*Ridiculous*
Fun	*Drunken*
Clever	*Two-faced*

STALKING THE DEAL

THE FIRST BUSINESS MEETING

When doing business, always wear a conservative dark suit with white shirt and blue tie. The Japanese are frightened by individualism. To them, a light blue shirt is rebellious and shocking.

One should never discuss business in the first business meeting. That would be considered rude and forward, even if you spent a year setting it up.

Pleased to meet you at last!	Yoyaku oai deki mashitane!	ようやく お会いでき ましたね！	*YO-ee-AH-koo oh-AI DEK-ee mosh-TA-nay!*
So sorry to disturb your busy schedule!	Ojama shite sumimasen!	お邪魔して すみません！	*Oh-JAH-ma SHEE-tay soo-mee-MA-sen!*
These are handsome offices.	Suteki na ofisu desune.	すてきな オフィスですね。	*Soo-TEK-ee na oh-FEE-soo dess-NAY.*
Say! How about those Tokyo Giants*/ Osaka Tigers!	Iya, jaiantsu/ taigasu no katsuyakuburi wa dodesu!	いやー、 ジャイアンツ／ タイガースの 活躍ぶりは どうです！	*EE-ya jai-AHN-tsu/tai-GA-soo no KAHT-so-YAH-koo-boo-ree wa doh-DESS!*
Quite a ball team!	Sugoi chimu desu yone!	すごいチーム ですよね！	*Soo-GOY CHEE-moo DAY-soo YO-nay!*

*Never mention the Giants outside of Tokyo.

STALKING THE DEAL

Well, we must be going.	Ah, mo shitsurei seneba narimasen.	あー、もう失礼せねばなりません。	*Ah, mo sheet-SOO-ray sen-AY-ba NAH-ree-MA-sen.*
We must catch a plane for our 20-hour, $3,000 flight home.	Ofuku yonjumanen haratta hikoki de, nijujikan kakete kaerimasu.	往復40万円払った飛行機で、20時間かけて帰ります。	*OAF-oo-koo yone-JOO-ma-nen ha-RA-tah hee-KOH-kee day, nee-JOO-jee-kahn ka-KAY-tay KAY-ree-MOSS.*
An honor to meet you!	Ome ni kakarete koei deshita!	お目にかかれて光栄でした！	*OH-may nee ka-ka-RAY-tay KOH-ay DESH-tah!*
We'll look you up again when we happen to find ourselves across the Pacific Ocean!	Moshi kochira ni kuru kikai ga areba mata yorasete itadaki masu!	もしこちらに来る機会があればまた寄らせていただきます！	*MOSH-ee ko-chee-ra nee KOO-roo kee-KAI ga ah-RAY-ba MA-tah YO-ra-SAY-tay ee-tah-DA-kee MOSS!*

SUMO-STYLE SALES TECHNIQUES

Sumo wrestling has direct parallels to business in Japan. Opponents test each other's character for what seems like ages, trying to gain psychological advantage, focusing on small details and avoiding direct confrontation. To the Japanese, a negotiation is like a *torikumi:* there's a winner and a loser.

The pushing and shoving of the final hours of negotiation are made of threats and ultimatums. Give as good as you get, and remember that the Japanese don't take ultimatums seriously.

I'm afraid we cannot accept your proposal.	Anata no goyobo niwa okotae dekikane masu.	あなたの御要望にはお応えできかねます。	*Ah-NAH-ta no go-yo-bo NEE-wa oh-KOH-tay DEK-ee-KAY-nay MOSS-en.*
We cannot return home with such a deal.	Sonna joken dewa kuni ewa kaeremasen.	そんな条件では、国へは帰れません。	*SO-nah jo-ken DAY-wa koo-nee AY-wa ka-AY-ray-MOSS-en.*
To lift the shame from our firm and families, we would all be forced to kill ourselves.	Shinde kaisha to kazoku ni owabi shimasu.	死んで会社と家族におわびします。	*SHIN-day KAI-shah toh ka-ZOKE nee oh-WA-bee shee-MOSS.*

STALKING THE DEAL

We offered you the moon.	Tsuki o kaimasenka.	月を買いませんか。	*TSOO-kee oh KAI-ma-SENK-ah.*
But you want Jupiter, Mars and Dolly Parton, too.	Mokusei to kasei to dori paton mo onozomi desuka.	木星と火星と、ドリー・パートンもお望みですか。	*MOKE-say toh ka-SAY toh doh-REE PAT-on mo own ZOH-me DESK-ah.*
Goodbye, gentlemen.	Sayonara minasan.	さようなら、みなさん。	*SIGH-oh-NAH-rah, MEE-nah-sahn.*
What? We misunder-stood?	EH? Gokai ga aru?	えっ？誤解がある？	*Eh? Go-KAI ga AH-roo?*
Fire the translator! Let's sit back down!	Tsuyaku o kubi ni shiro! Mo ichido hanashiai masho!	通訳をクビにしろ！もう一度話し合いましょう！	*TSOO-ya-koo oh koo-bee nee SHEE-roh! Mo ee-CHEE-doh ha-NAH-shee-AI ma-SHO!*

INTERPRETING NON-VERBAL SIGNALS

Just as the Japanese language is different from our own, so are the hand gestures and facial expressions.

SIGNAL	MEANING
A sharp, exhaling breath and a breaking of eye contact.	*"I find it hard to accept or understand what you are saying."*
Smiling.	*"You make me uncomfortable."*
Long, stone-faced silence.	*"We are considering your proposal."*
Even longer silence.	*"Don't rush us."*
Snoring.	*"Your deadline approaches, yes?"*
Shaking finger at someone.	*"I have hostile feelings."*
Pointing finger at own chest.	*"I want to fight you."*
Coming across table, shouting, "Tawake!"	*"Your proposal is not pleasing."*

NEVER JUST SAY NO

Japanese negotiators will test you by asking for unilateral concessions. DO NOT GIVE IN. The smallest unilateral concession will convince your opponents that you are the moral equivalent of a sea cucumber, fit not for battle but for soup.

Still, since harmony must be preserved at all costs, you must never say no. You can use the Japanese method of stonewalling—appearing to agree but not giving anything away—or use phrases like these.

Good idea.	Ee kangae desu.	いい考えです。	*ee KON-gay gay DAY-soo.*
You are very generous.	Goshinsetsu arigato.	御親切 ありがとう。	*GO-shin-SET-soo AH-ree-GA-toh.*
I will be happy to reveal trade secrets for free.	Tada de shobai no himitsu o ooshie shimasho.	タダで、商売の 秘密を教え ましょう。	*TA-da day sho-BAI no hee-MEET-soo oh OH-shee SHEE-ma-SHOW.*
It would certainly excite my colleagues back home.	Kore o kuni no doryo ga kiitara bikkuri shimasu.	これを国の 同僚が聞いたら ビックリします。	*KOH-ray oh KOO-nee no DOOR-ee-oh ga kee-TA-rah BEE-koo-ree shee-MOSS.*

(continued)

STALKING THE DEAL

Change the meeting time by 10 minutes?	Miitingu no jikan o juppun henkou suruno desuka?	ミーティングの時間を10分変更するのですか？	*MEE-teen-goo no jee-KAHN oh joo-POON hen-KOH soo-ROO-no DESK-ah.*
My colleagues are certain to like that idea.	Dooryo mo yoi an dato iukoto desho.	同僚も良い案だという事でしょう。	*DOH-ree-yoh mo yoy ahn DA-toh YOO-koh-toh DESH-oh.*
I will consult with them.	Minato soudan itashimasu.	皆と相談いたします。	*Mee-NA-toh SO-dahn EE-ta-shee-MA-soo.*
Then I will arrange a conference call to get permission from my superiors at the home office.	Honsha no uwayaku karano kyokka o erutameno denwa o kakemasho.	本社の上役からの許可を得るための電話をかけましょう。	*HONE-shah no OO-wa-YA-koo ka-RA-no KYO-ka oh ay-roo-TA-may-no DEN-wa oh ka-kay-ma-SHOW.*
When shall we meet to discuss your time-change proposal?	Jikan no henkou ni tsuite itsu oaishite hanase-masuka?	時間の変更について何時にお会いして話せますか？	*Jee-KAHN no hen-KO nee TSOO-ee-tay EET-soo oh-AYSH-tay HA-nah-say-MOSS-kah?*

THE INEVITABLE THANK-YOU NOTE

Experienced travelers write thank-you notes to people they meet on their journeys. This common courtesy increases international understanding and leads to the all-important trust necessary to murder the Japanese in business dealings.

Thank you for the tour of Tokyo.	Tokyo no annai arigato gozaimashita.	東京の案内、ありがとうございました。	*TOH-kee-OH no ah-NAI AH-ree-GA-toh GO-zai-MOSH-ta.*
The Toyota building was impressive.	Toyota birudingu wa sugokatta.	豊田ビルディングはすごかった。	*Toh-yo-ta BEE-roo-DEEN-goo wa SOO-go-KA-ta.*
It is very large!	Okindakara!	大きいんだから！	*OH-keen-da-KA-rah.*
The Imperial Palace was also interesting.	Kokyo mo subarashi katta.	皇居もすばらしかった。	*KO-kee-oh mo SOO-ba-RAH-shee KA-ta.*
Amazing that plants can grow in Tokyo air!	Tokyo no kuki demo shokubutsu ga sodatsu nante odoroki desu!	東京の空気でも植物が育つなんて、驚きです！	*TOH-kee-OH no koo-kee DAY-mo SHO-koo-BOOTS ga so-DOT-soo NON-tay oh-doh-ROH-kee DESS!*

(continued)

STALKING THE DEAL

And I was excited to visit McDonald's.	Makudonarudo ni ittanowa wasureraremasen.	マクドナルドに行ったのは忘れられません。	*MA-koo-DON-oh-ROO-doh nee EE-ta-NO-wa wa-SOO-ray-ray-ree-MOSS-en.*
What a perceptive and amazing host you are!	Anata wa nante mehashi no kiku motenashi-yaku dattano desho!	あなたは何て目端の効くもてなし役だったのでしょう！	*Ah-NAH-tah wa NON-tay mee-HA-shee no KEE-koo mo-ten-AH-shee-YA-koo da-TA-no desh!*
How did you know I liked burgers and fries?	Doshite watashi ga hanbaga to poteto no sukinakoto ga wakari mashitaka?	どうして私がハンバーガーとポテトの好きな事がわかりましたか？	*DOH-shee-tay wa-TOSH ga han-BA-GA toh poh-TAY-toh no SOO-kee-na-KOH-toh ga wa-KA-ree mosh-TA-kah?*
Thanks again for all the thrills.	Omoshiroi taiken, domo arigato gozaimashita.	面白い体験、どうもありがとうございました。	*OH-mo-shee-ROY TAI-ken, DOH-mo AH-ree-GA-toh GO-zai-MOSH-ta.*
Your servant,	Anata no shimobe,	あなたの僕、	*ah-NAH-tah no shee-MO-bay,*

Wicked
SPANISH

Si me amas, mi frijolito refrito, traime el termómetro.

It you love me, my little refried bean, fetch the thermometer.

See may AH-mas, mee free-ho-LEE-toh ray-FREE-toh, tra-EE-meh el ter-MOH-may-troh.

CONTENTS

THE MODEL GUEST

HELP

DAILY LIFE

CULTURE

BIENVENIDO

Travel in Spanish-speaking countries means more than cheap hotels and quick suntans—one must adapt to foreign customs and attitudes. To the uninitiated, Hispanic culture can be confusing and frustrating.

Our forms of logic, efficiency, and refrigeration are largely unknown. Other things we take for granted are rare or nonexistent, including clearly marked prices, paved roads, and college-educated waitresses.

We may be startled by pigs as they run through the streets or hang over the sidewalk. We may be terrified by blind taxi drivers. We may be baffled when locals fail to respond to wads of cash waved in the air.

In some ways, we gringos see the world so differently that we live in what's almost a separate

reality. While we're dividing every day into hours, every hour into minutes and every minute into 60 perfect little seconds, for example, they're wondering what kind of fool would spend three thousand bucks on a watch.

As we wait another half-hour for a waiter to show up, they try to conserve their energy for a two-and-a-half-hour dinner that will begin sometime after 11 PM.

And as we absolutely insist on an immediate upgrade to the El Presidente suite, they're wondering what we'll look like after we've been dead for five or six hundred years.

Naïve, unprepared travelers feel angry, humiliated, and, most of all, baffled. But Wicked Travelers never seem to suffer. They always appear to be at ease, even when they have no clue what's going to happen next.

They have an intuitive understanding of life abroad and a special sensitivity for alien cultures and ideas. They are also heavily armed. Not with gold cards, loud voices, or idle threats in English, but with warm smiles, patient attitudes, and a variety of verbal weapons that natives understand.

Buena suerte!

THE OLD MAN AND THE CHEVY

The mañana concept is a paradox of Hispanic culture. While the clerks and waiters of an entire nation may appear to be in a collective coma, the taxi drivers seem to run on crystal meth.

The antiquity of many taxis only adds to the terror of high-speed rides. But before you resort to violence or leap from the vehicle, try a little verbal persuasion.

This car is amazing.	Este carro es increíble.	*Es-tay CA-roh ehs in-kray-EE-blay.*
I never knew chicken wire had so many uses.	Yo no sabía que la tela metálica tenía tantos usos.	*Yoh noh sah-BEE-ah kay la TAY-la meh-TAH-lee-kah ten-EE-ah TAHN-tohs OOS-ohs.*
When did the brakes go out?	¿Cuándo se fueron los frenos?	*KWAN-doh say fooEH-ron los FREH-nos?*
In the Eisenhower years?	¿En la época de Carranza?	*En la ay-POH-kah day cah-RONZ-ah?*

Please give us helmets/ blindfolds.	Por favor dénos cascos/unas vendas para los ojos.	*Pohr fah-VOAR DAY-nohs KAHS-kohs/OON-ahs VAIN-das PAH-rah los OH-hoes.*
Look, if you don't slow down, I won't pay you.	Mire, si no reduce la velocidad, no le voy a pagar.	*MEER-ay, see noh reh-doo-seh la vay-LO-see-DOD, no leh voee ah pah-gahr.*
That's much better, thanks.	Mucho mejor, gracias.	*MOO-cho meh-HORE, GRAH-see-ahs.*

DISCLAIMER OF WICKEDNESS

In consideration of 1) the explosive tempers engendered by the combined effects of hot weather, hotter food, and the Laws of Machismo, and 2) the insensitivity of certain Americans abroad, combined with said travelers' wrenching pronunciation and deeply mistaken sense of invulnerability, the author and his assigns, agents, bodyguards, pallbearers and heirs hereby disclaim, categorically deny and strangle at birth all claims and actions arising from the use, misuse, or failure to use any of the words, phrases, strategies, or attitudes contained in this volume.

STOP BUS!

Buses are great travel bargains. For seventeen cents you can go twenty miles and feel like you've gone two hundred.

Oxygen may be scarce inside; either find a window seat or join the economy class passengers clinging to the colorfully painted exterior of the vehicle.

Memorize these basic bus-travel phrases.

Yours is the prettiest piglet, miss.	Su cochinito es el más lindo, señorita.	*Soo co-chee-NEE-toh ehs el mahs LEEN-doh, SEE-nyoh-REE-tah.*
But it has shat in my lap.	Pero se me ha cagado en las piernas.	*PAIR-oh say meh ha cah-GAH-doh en lahs pee-AIR-nahs.*
The cliffs are very steep.	Los acantilados son muy empinados.	*Los ah-kan-tee-LA-dohs sohn moo-EE em-pee-nah-dos.*
The bus is very fast.	El camión es muy rápido.	*El cam-YONE ehs moo-EE RAH-pee-doh.*
Do I smell an old enchilada?	¿Acaso huelo una enchilada vieja?	*Ah-CAH-soh WHAY-loh OO-nah EN-chee-LAH-dah vee-AY-ha?*
I don't feel well.	No me siento bien.	*No may see-EN-toh bee-EN.*

| **Please lend me your hat.** | Por favor, préstame su sombrero. | *Pohr fah-VOAR PRES-tah-may soo som-BRAY-roh.* |

PRAYER OF THE LOST LUGGAGE

O mighty Zapoletoltecoaxacoatlototoc, God of Flight, Locusts and Lost Luggage, please return to me my handsome Gucci bag that went to Guadalajara or Guadalupe. I dare not make a pilgrimage to your Holy Rockpile without the brand-new matching outfit from Bergdorf's contained in said Gucci bag. And if you can spare a moment from your busy schedule, O Winged Reptilian Unhappiness, please firmly spite all cruel and inept baggage handlers.

O poderoso Zapoletoltecoaxacoatlototoc, Dios de la Aviación, Langostas y Equipaje Perdido, por favor a regrésame mi elegante maleta Gucci que fue a parar a Guadalajara o Guadalupe. No me atrevo a hacer un peregrinaje a tu santo montón de piedras sin mi nuevo traje de Bergdorf's contenido dentro de tal maleta Gucci. Y si pudieras darme un minuto de tu valioso tiempo, O Infelicidad Reptilia y Alada, por favor castiga severamente a todo cruel e inepto maletero.

ADDRESSING THE MULE

I f you are ever required to ride a mule or burro, you should have the satisfaction of addressing it in its own tongue. Keep in mind, however, that while all pack animals understand Spanish, none follow directions.

Sweetheart. Darling. Move!	Cariño. Querida. ¡Muévete!	*Cah-REE-nyoh. Kay-REE-dah. MWAIVE-ay-tay!*
I'm talking to you.	Te estoy hablando.	*Tay ess-TOY ah-BLAHN-doh.*
I've seen turds more energetic than you!	¡Yo he visto mojones más enérgicos que tú!	*Yoh ay VEES-toh moh-HOH-nehs mahs eh-NEHR-hee-kohs kay too!*
And I've had enough of your noisy complaints!	¡Y ya basta de tus quejas escandalosas!	*Ee yah BAHS-tah day toos KAY-hahs ehs-kahn-dah-LOH-sahs!*
I will not negotiate.	No negociaré.	*No nay-GOH-see-ah-RAY.*
Shall I beat you to within an inch of your life?	¿Acaso quieres que te dé una paliza hasta el borde de la muerte?	*Ah-KAH-soh kee-AIR-ace kay tay day OO-nah pah-LEE-zah AHS-tah el BOR-day la MWER-tay?*

| Whoa! I said whoa! Pretty please, whoa! | ¡Alto! ¡Dije alto! ¡Por favorcito, alto! | *AHL-toh! DEE-hay AHL-toh! Pohr-fah-voar-SEE-toh AHL-toh!* |

CUSTOMS TIPS

The wide variety of contraband available south of the border provides jobs for thousands of U.S. Customs agents. They don't necessarily want to arrest you, but they are trusted to protect the border. And they love to slap handcuffs on smugglers and left-wing liberals. Adjusting your appearance may speed your border crossing.

BAD	BETTER	BEST
Surfboard	*Sailboard*	Tennis racquet
Huraches	*Reeboks*	Loafers
Drawstring Pants	*Jeans*	Starched chinos
Tie-dyed T-shirt	*Polo shirt*	Brooks Brothers' button-down
Sunglasses	*No glasses*	Thick glasses
Volkswagen van	*Dodge mini-van*	Forty-foot RV
Old Volvo	*New Buick*	New Volvo

TIPPING POLICEMEN

When Mexico City's chief of police was asked how he could build a $2.5 million mansion on his $65 a week salary, he said he saved carefully and made wise investments. He didn't mention the tradition of *la mordida*, "the little bite."

Any visitor driving a car is likely to get bitten, but a "tip" will not always free one from the jaws of injustice. Some policemen want to accept money *and* preserve their honor.

What seems to be the problem, officer?	¿Cuál es el problema, oficial?	*Kwal ehs ehl pro-BLEH-mah, oh-fee-si-AL?*
The light was quite green, actually.	En realidad, el semáforo estaba en verde.	*En ray-AL-ee-DAHD, el seh-MAH-fo-roh ehs-TAH-bah ehn VAIR-day.*
No, I am not calling you a liar.	No, yo no lo estoy llamando mentiroso.	*No, yoh no lo ess-TOY yah-MAHN-doh men-tee-ROH-soh.*
I'm sure we can work this out.	Estoy seguro que podemos arreglar esto.	*Ess-TOY say-GOO-roh kay poh-DEH-mohs ah-re-GLAHR ESH-toh.*
Here are my papers.	Aquí están mis papeles.	*Ah-KEE es-TAHN meece pah-PEH-lehs.*

Would these green papers help?	¿Servirían también estos papelitos verdes?	*Sair-vee-REE-ahn tahm-bee-EN EHS-tohs PAH-peh-lee-tohs VAIR-dehs?*
Do you need so many of them?	¿Acaso necesita tantos?	*Ah-CAH-so nay-say-SEE-tah TAHN-tos?*
Do the handcuffs have to be so tight?	¿Tienen que estar tan apretadas las esposas?	*Tee-EH-nen kay ess-TAR tahn ah-pray-TAH-dahs las ess-POH-sahs?*

GETTING AROUND

PEDESTRIAN ADVISORY

Local drivers will display behavior different from what you're used to at home. The chart below shows typical Latino driving speeds under assorted conditions.

TERRAIN	PREFERRED SPEED	
	MPH	KPH
Thick Jungle	50	80
High Brush	55	90
Rabbit Trail	65	105
Footpath	70	110
Cliff Edge in Thunderstorm	95	155
Sidewalk	100	160
Super Highway	110	175
Paved Super Highway	55	90
City Street	15	25

Note: No driver will slow for red lights or oncoming vehicles, lest he be considered weak and feminine.

ROAD SIGNS

If you must drive, memorize the road signs unique to Spanish-speaking countries.

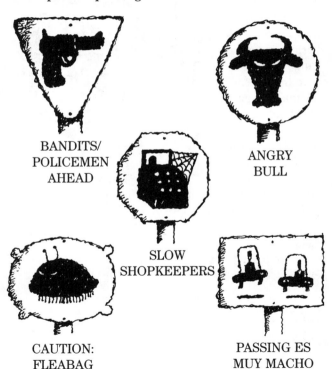

BANDITS/
POLICEMEN
AHEAD

ANGRY
BULL

SLOW
SHOPKEEPERS

CAUTION:
FLEABAG
HOTELS

PASSING ES
MUY MACHO
NEXT 5 KM

DESTINATIONS

SURVIVING THE HOTEL

Old hotels—and that includes most of them—may have a wide variety of rooms, ranging from revolting to barely adequate. Never check into a hotel before looking at the room you are to be given. And don't rely on a guidebook for the nightly rate; inflation can raise prices in a matter of hours.

Could I see a couple of rooms, please?	¿Podría ver un par de cuartos por favor?	*Poh-DREE-ah vair oon par day KWAR-tohs pohr fah-VOAR?*
I understand this building is 400 years old.	Entiendo que este edificio tiene cuatrocientos años.	*En-tee-EN-doh kay EHS-tay eh-dee-FEECE-ee-yoh tee-EN-ay KWAH-troh-see-EN-tohs AHN-yohs.*

Is that the original paint/maid?	¿Es esta la pintura/sirvienta original?	*Ehs EHS-tah lah peen-TOO-rah/seer-VEE-ehn-tah oh-REE-jeen-nahl?*
How authentic!	¡Qué auténtico!	*Kay ow-TEN-tee-koh!*
I don't mind the spiders.	No me molestan las arañas.	*No may moh-LES-tahn las ah-RAHN-yahs.*
But I'd prefer a room without scorpions.	Pero preferiría una habitación sin alacranes.	*PAIR-oh PRAY-fair-eer-REE-ah OO-nah ah-bee-tah-see-OHN seen ah-lah-KRAH-nehss.*
Is there a room that doesn't face the bus station/ mescal bar/ slaughterhouse?	¿Tiene alguna habitación que no dé a la estación de camiones/cantina/matadero?	*Tee-EH-nay ahl-GOO-nah ah-bee-tah-see-OHN kay no DAY ah la ehs-tah-see-OHN day kah-mee-OH-nayss/cahn-TEE-nah/mah-tah-DARE-oh?*
Is there a room with a window/ bathroom?	¿Tiene alguna habitación con ventana/baño?	*Tee-EH-nay ahl-GOO-nah ah-bee-tah-see-OHN con ven-TAH-nah/BAHN-yoh?*
Is there another hotel in this town?	¿Hay otro hotel en esta ciudad?	*Ah-ee OH-troh oh-TEL en EHS-tah see-oo-DAHD?*

WHEN IN RUINS

A trip to Mexico or Peru wouldn't be complete without a visit to ancient ruins. They're inspiring and mysterious, partly because you won't find an "interpretive center" or signs explaining the various features.

If you want to hire a guide, interview several candidates before selecting one. Many historical facts have been lost; look for a guide with a vivid imagination.

If your Spanish isn't very good, you may want to test candidates by asking these questions in English.

Who is depicted in that carving?	¿Quién está representado en ese grabado?	*Kee-EN es-TAH rep-ray-zen-TAH-doh en EH-say grah-BAH-doh?*
What happened to his heart/ head/genitals?	¿Qué pasó con su corazón/cabeza/ órganos?	*Kay pah-SOH kohn soo coh-rah-ZOHN/ cah-BAYS-ah/ OR-gah-nohs?*
My friend, you are a sick man.	Amigo, usted está mal de la cabeza.	*Ah-MEE-goh, oos-TED ehs-TAH mahl day la cah-BAY-sah.*
You're hired.	Queda contratado.	*KAY-dah kohn-trah-TAH-doh.*

UNDERSTANDING ZAPOTEC BASKETBALL

Visiting ancient sites is more enjoyable when you know their history. Small stadiums are central features of many Mexican ruins, and as your guide will explain, a sport like basketball was played there. Here are a few details about the game.

HOW POINTS WERE SCORED

One Point: Putting Ball Through Hoop, Holding, Shoving

Two Points: Clubbing, Stabbing, Blinding

Three Points: Dismembering, Disemboweling, Decapitating

FAVORITE TEAMS OF THE SMALL TEN

- Gourd Valley College Rain Gods
- Feathered Serpent School High Priests
- Primitive State Cougar-Catchers
- Jungle University Poisonous Mushrooms

NECESSARY EQUIPMENT

- Obsidian Knives
- Feather Shields
- Granite Balls
- Coffins

THE PLAYERS

Average Height: Four feet, four inches

Average Weight: 90 pounds

Average Length of Career: Six minutes

DESTINATIONS

CONFESSION

A town's finest architecture, painting and sculpture are often found at the cathedral. Best of all, the thick stone walls provide natural air-conditioning on hot afternoons.

Forgive me, Father.	Perdóneme, Padre.	*Pair-DOH-nay-may, PAH-dray.*
I have never confessed before in my life.	Nunca me he confesado antes en mi vida.	*NOON-ka may eh kohn-feh-SAH-doh AHN-tehss en mee VEE-dah.*
In fact, I don't intend to now.	Ni tampoco pienso hacerlo ahora.	*Nee tam-POH-koh pee-EN-soh ah-SAIR-loh ah-OHR-ah.*
I came in here to get out of the sun.	Entré aquí para resguardarme del sol.	*Ehn-TRAY ah-KEE PAH-rah ress-GWARD-ahr-may del sol.*
How about those Padres?	¿Y qué tal los Padres de San Diego?	*Ee kay tahl los PAH-drays day sahn dee-AY-goh?*
You're right. Their relief pitching is a little weak.	Tiene razón. Los relevistas están un poco flojos.	*Tee-EN-ay rah-ZOHN. Los ray-lay-VEES-tahs ehs-TAHN oon POH-koh FLO-hohs.*

Maybe they need a little help from above.	Quizás necesiten un poco de ayuda del cielo.	*Kee-ZAHS nay-say-SEE-ten oon POH-koh day ah-YOO-dah del see-AY-loh.*
Shall we pray?	¿Rezamos?	*Ray-SAH-mohs?*

DEATH TAKES A HOLIDAY

Mexicans remind themselves of fate and fore-bears during the Days of the Dead, which begin on Halloween. Families make special altars and honor deceased members with gifts of food, cigarettes and liquor.

On the evening of November 2, people parade in costumes and skulls to the graveyard for a picnic with dead relatives. Children get skeleton dolls and candy skulls with their names printed on the foreheads. Local artisans will be happy to depict you and your family as you will look after you are dead. Join the colorful cere-monies, but:

• Do not offer to nail anyone's coffin shut;
• Do not consume offerings meant for the dead, tequila in particular;
• Do not make offerings of money or Kaopectate;
• Do not tell dead waiters to hurry up.

FINDING THE MUSEUM

The trouble with Latino museums is finding them. Everyone you ask for directions will want you to see the best parts of town on your way to your destination. You may need to ask for directions several times.

Direct us to the Museum of Fine Arts/ Anthropology.	Diríjanos al museo de Bellas Artes/ Antropología.	*Dee-REE-hah-nos al moo-SAY-oh day BELL-yahss AR-tays/ ahn-troh-poh-loh-HEE-ah.*
Left at the church, left at the plaza and left at the hundred-year-old beggar?	¿A la izquierda en la iglesia, izquierda en la plaza, y a la izquierda en el limosnero de cien años?	*Ah la ees-kee-AIR-dah en la ee-GLAY-see-ah, ees-kee-AIR-dah en la PLAH-sah, ee ah la ees-kee-AIR-dah en el lee-mohs-NAY-roh day see-EN AHN-yohs?*
Is there another way?	¿Hay alguna otra ruta?	*Eye ahl-GOO-nah OH-trah ROO-tah?*
We've met the beggar several times already.	Pero si ya pasamos por el limosnero varias veces.	*PAIR-oh see yah pah-SAH-mohs pohr el lee-mohs-NAY-roh VAH-ree-ahss VEH-says.*

Okay, let me get this straight.	Bueno, permítame que lo entienda.	*BWAY-noh, pair-MEE-tah-may kay loh ehn-tee-EN-dah.*
Right at the iron gate, right on the paved road, right at the meat market, and right at the fried dough seller.	A la derecha en la reja de hierro, a la derecha en el camino pavimentado, a la derecha en el mercado de carne, y a la derecha en el vendedor de churros.	*Ah la dah-RAY-cha en lah RAY-ha day YEH-roh, ah lah da-RAY-cha en el kah-MEE-noh pah-vee-men-TAH-doh, ah la dah-RAY-cha en el mair-KAH-doh day CAR-nay, ee ah la da-RAY-cha en el ven-day-DOHR day CHOO-rahs.*
Thanks very much. We are sure to find it now.	Muchas gracias. Seguro que lo encontramos ahora.	*Moo-chahs GRAH-see-ahs. Say-GOO-roh kay loh en-con-TRAH-mohs ah-oh-ra.*

BEACH BLANKET LINGO

The vendors wandering along Latin American beaches are not marketing experts. You can help them by explaining your needs as a consumer.

Yes, madam, that is a beautiful wool serape.	Sí, señora, ése es un lindo serape de lana.	*See, seen-YOHR-ah, EH-say ehs oon LEEN-doh sah-RAH-pay day LAH-nah.*
The burro motif is appealing.	El motivo con el burro es interesante.	*El moh-TEE-voh kohn ehl BOO-roh ehs ehn-tair-eh-SAHN-tay.*
But it is 95 degrees here on the beach.	Pero hace treinta y cinco grados aquí en la playa.	*PAIR-oh AH-seh TRAIN-tah ee SEEN-koh GRAH-dos ah-KEY en lah PLAH-yah.*
I do not need 10 pounds of wool today.	No necesito cuatro kilos de tela de lana hoy.	*No nay-say-SEE-toh KWAH-troh KEE-lohs day TAY-lah day LAH-nah OH-ee.*
Have you got any cold beer?	¿Tiene cerveza fría?	*Tee-EN-ay sair-VAY-sah FREE-ah?*

ATTENTION THIRD-WORLD SHOPPERS

The excellent produce and handmade items of the less-industrialized world may seem like bargains. But before buying anything—and especially before bringing it home—consider the hazards.

ITEM	BENEFIT	DRAWBACK
Wooden mask	*Looks great in den or playroom.*	Tiny insects eat mask, make home in den or playroom.
Sombrero	*Authentic replica of actual hat.*	Can't be packed; looks ridiculous on plane ride.
Assorted produce	*Lots of flavor for pennies a serving.*	Rinse in local water may add typhus germs.
Piñata	*Bright colors, fun for kids.*	Certain to be torn in half at border by customs agents.
Marijuana	*Almost free, mind-blowing.*	"Making friends" in a sweaty Mexican prison.
Heroin	*Super-discount, 95% pure.*	Being shot at dawn in a sweaty Mexican prison.

RESTAURANT SURVIVAL TECHNIQUES

I t is painful to watch your brief vacation evaporate while waiters and waitresses smoke, chat, hang out, and nap.

They are not trying to irritate you. They merely want to make your meal more delicious. Just before dawn, when the food is served, it will seem like a blessing, no matter how lousy it is. A few phrases may help move things along.

I feel faint!	¡Me desmayo!	*May dess-MAI-oh!*
My blood pressure is dropping!	¡Me está bajando la presión!	*May ehs-TAH bah-HAN-doh lah preh-see-YOHN!*
Help! Emergency!	¡Socorro! ¡Emergencia!	*Soh-KOH-rroh! Eh-mair-HEN-see-ah!*
Is there a waiter in the house?	¿Hay un mesero aquí?	*Ay oon may-SARE-oh ah-KEE?*
Are you a waiter/waitress? Thank God!	¿Es usted un/una mesero/mesera? ¡Gracias a Dios!	*Ehs oos-TED ooon/oon-ah may-SARE-oh/may-SARE-ah? GRAH-see-ahs ah DEE-ohs!*
Forget the menu!	¡Olvidese de la carta!	*Ole-VEE-day-say day la CAR-tah!*

SUSTENANCE

Just show me to your kitchen.	Sólo muéstreme su cocina.	*So-loh MWAY-stray-may soo koh-SEE-nah.*
I'll help myself.	Me sirvo solo.	*May-SEER-voh so-loh.*
But you might as well take my breakfast order now.	Más vale que tome mi orden del desayuno ahora.	*Mass VAH-lay kay TOH-may mee OR-den del des-seye-OO-noh ah-OR-ah.*

LOOK OUT FOR "CHICKEN OF THE TREES"

L atin cuisine includes hundreds of unusual dishes, but visitors may not want to taste them all. "Chicken of the trees," for example, is an iguana. Still, there is sure to be something nourishing and bland on the menu. Learn how to ask for it by name.

What lies motionless under the spicy chocolate sauce?	¿Qué yace immóvil dentro del mole?	*Kay YAH-say imm-MOH-veel DEN-troh del MOH-lay?*
What oozes from the depths of the stuffed pepper?	¿Qué emana de las profundidades del chile relleno?	*Kay ay-MAH-nah day las proh-foon-dee-DAH-days del CHEE-lay ray-YAY-noh?*
What stares at me with glassy eyes?	¿Qué es lo que me mira con ojos vidriosos?	*Kay ehs loh kay may MEER-ah con OH-hohs vee-dree-OH-sohs?*
Ah. I had that last night.	Ah. Comí eso anoche.	*Ah. Coh-MEE EH-soh ah-NOH-chay.*
That is an unusually large octopus.	Ese pulpo es extraordinaria-mente grande.	*Eh-seh POOL-poh ehs eks-trah-or-dee-nah-ree-ah-MEN-tay GRAHN-day.*

Is it the same one that was on display yesterday?	¿Es acaso el mismo que vimos expuesto ayer?	*Ehs ah-CHA-soh el MEEZ-moh kay BEE-mos eks-PWEST-oh ah-YAIR?*
Perhaps by now it is ripe.	Quizás ya esté maduro.	*Kee-SAHS yah ehs-teh mah-DOO-rah.*
How are the rice and beans this evening?	¿Qué tal están el arroz y frijoles esta noche?	*Kay tahl ehs-TAHN ehl ah-ROHS ee free-HOLE-ehs EHS-tah NOH-chay?*

GUIDE TO PAINLESS DINING

Contrary to popular belief, extremely hot foods are not good for you. That is why they hurt so much. People who like to dine in pain will enjoy eating in Mexico. But those who prefer non-toxic dishes will also find appealing items on the menu.

I love hot food.	Me encanta la comida picante.	*May en-KAHN-tah la koh-MEE-dah pee-KAHN-tay.*
But I ate a serrano pepper last week.	Pero comí un chile serrano la semana pasada.	*PAIR-oh coh-MEE oon CHEE-lay sair-AH-noh la say-MAH-nah pah-SAH-dah.*
It really opened my eyes!	¡En verdad me abrió los ojos!	*En vair-DAD may ah-bree-OH los OH-hohs!*
And it lost none of its potency passing through my body.	Y no perdió nada de su potencia al pasar por mi organismo.	*Ee no pair-dee-DOH NAH-dah day soo poh-TEN-see-ah ahl pah-SAR pohr mee or-gah-NEEZ-moh.*
The swelling is going down now.	La hinchazón ya se me está pasando.	*La EEN-cha-sohn yaa say may ehs-TAH pah-SAHN-doh.*
The blisters will heal soon.	Las ampollas se curarán pronto.	*Las ahm-POLL-yahs say KOO-rah-RAHN PROHN-toh.*

But for now, dry toast will be fine.	Pero por ahora, pan tostado sin mantequilla.	*PAIR-oh pohr ah-OR-ah, pahn toss-TAH-doh seen MAN-tay-KEE-ah.*

PRAYER OF THE LARGE INTESTINE

O Saint Elena the Rather Plump, I beg your favor to punish and kill the Devils that have taken adverse possession of my normally rugged digestive system. And, O Thunder Thighs, I have lost fifteen pounds in the last three days and would be willing to make a special pilgrimage every year to your shrine in Cancún if I do not gain this weight back, your Holy Circumference.

O Santa Elena la Regordeta, te ruego el favor de castigar y matar a los Diabólicos que se han apoderado adversamente de mi normalmente sano aparato digestivo. Y, O Piernas Estruendosas, he perdido siete kilos en los últimos tres días y estaré dispuesto(a) a hacer un peregrinaje especial cada año a tu templo en Cancún si no recupero estos kilos de nuevo, O Bendita Circunferencia.

THE MEN-ONLY BAR

O n a hot afternoon, few things satisfy like a cold *cerveza* and a few handfuls of salty chips. In smaller towns, however, tradition may hold that drinking establishments are for men only. The few women in such places are assumed to be for hire. You may feel a need to make a general announcement to avoid misunderstanding and injury.

Excuse me, gentlemen.	¡Discúlpenme, caballeros!	*Dees-KOOL-pen-may, CAH-bah-YAIR -ohs!*
I'd like to make an announcement.	Me gustaría hacer un anuncio.	*May goos-tah-REE-ah ah-SAIR oon ah-NOON-see-oh.*
This is my wife.	Esta es mi esposa.	*EHS-tah ehs mee ess-POH-sah.*
She is from a good family.	Es de buena familia.	*Ehs day BWAY-nah fah-MEEL-ee-ah.*
Do not stare at her.	No la miren.	*No lah MEE-ren.*
Do not touch her.	No la toquen.	*No lah TOH-ken.*
We are here for the beer.	Estamos aquí por la cerveza.	*Ehs-TAH-mohs ah-KEE pohr la sair-VAY-sah.*

FOR WOMEN ONLY: COIN-A-CURSE

Alone woman may be the object of rude comments from Spanish-speaking men. The best response is silence, but some victims insist on counter-attack.

Create your own invective from the columns below. Adjectives follow nouns. Begin with a word from column C and add words from A and B, as in *rata de al cantarilla incontinente sin dientes* (toothless incontinent sewer rat).

A	B	C
filthy cochino *co-CHEE-noh*	**polyester-clad** revestido en poliester *reh-VEHS-tee-doh ehn POH-lee-ES-tair*	**butcher boy** niño carnicero *NEEN-yoh CAR-nee-SAY-roh*
toothless sin dientes *seen dee-EN-tays*	**incontinent** incontinente *in-CON-teen-EN-tay*	**sewer rat** rata de al cantarilla *RA-tah day al KAN-tah-ree-yah*
cretinous cretino *cray-TEE-noh*	**ill-bred** malnacido *mahl-nah-SEED-oh*	**maggot-mouth** boca de gusano *BOH-kah day goo-SAH-noh*
squirming retorcido *ray-TOHR-see-doh*	**frog-lipped** labios de sapo *LAH-bee-ohs deh SAH-poh*	**midget** enano *ay-NOH-noh*

Note: Men who value their lives should never utter these phrases.

SUSTENANCE

DRINKING TO KILL THE CRITTERS WITHIN

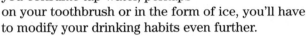

Try to drink only bottled fluids. Do not accept bottles that have been opened out of sight. If you consume tap water, perhaps on your toothbrush or in the form of ice, you'll have to modify your drinking habits even further.

Bartender! A Pepto Bismol, straight up!	¡Barman! ¡Un Pepto Bismol solo!	*BAHR-mahn! Oon PEHP-toh BEEZ-mahl so-loh!*
I am very grateful. And now, a toast!	Se lo agradezco mucho. ¡Y ahora un brindis!	*Say loh ah-grah-DAYS-koh MOO-choh. Ee ah-OR-ah oon brin-DEES!*
To the eternal suffering of a certain restaurateur!	¡Al eterno sufrimiento de cierto dueño de restaurante!	*Ahl ay-TARE-noh soo-free-mee-EN-toh day see-AIR-toh DWAIN-yoh day res-taw-RAHN-tay!*
May large armadillos copulate in his colon!	¡Ojalá que enormes armadillos copulen en sus intestinos!	*Oh-hah-LAH kay ay-NOR-mays AR-mah-DEEL-yohs koh-poo-len een sus in-tes-TEE-nohs!*

May flames shoot from between his cheeks!	¡Ojalá que dispare llamas por el culo!	*Oh-hah-LAH kay diss-PAH-ray YAH-mahs pohr ehl koo-loh!*
May he eat his own cooking and croak!	¡Ojalá que coma su propia comida y muera!	*Oh-hah-LAH kay COH-mah soo PRO-pee-ah koh-MEE-dah ee MWARE-ah!*

MEXICAN DRINKS OF DEATH

equila is a potent liquor made from cactus. It tastes so awful that many people lick salt and suck on a lime after each swallow. The more obscure brands of tequila should be sipped through your clenched teeth, carefully straining out the sand, twigs, and insect parts.

Mescal is a mildly hallucinogenic liquor also made from cactus. It adds a fresh, unpredictable element to any drunken afternoon. If drinking mescal fails to make you violently ill, try chewing on the dead worm at the bottom of your bottle.

Pulque is made by *pulqueños* who chew on cactus, spit into a jar and let the mixture sit for a few weeks. Beer is okay for some people, but it takes a real man to drink a warm glass of fermented Mexican spit.

MOCTEZUMA'S MEDICAL EMERGENCY

No matter how careful you are, you will probably get sick during your visit. When the agony overtakes you, there are two things to remember: 1) Nobody lives forever; 2) Local doctors will do everything in their power to make your last hours on earth as painful and unpleasant as possible.

I ate/drank something in your country.	Comí/bebí algo en su país.	*Coh-MEE/bay-BEE AHL-goh en soo pah-EES.*
Please call a priest/travel agent.	Por favor llame a un cura/agente de viajes.	*Pohr fah-VOAR YAH-may ah oon COO-rah /ah-HEN-tay day vee-AH-hays.*
I would like to make a will/ receive last rites.	Me gustaría hacer un testamento/ recibir extremaunción.	*May goos-tah-REE-ah ah-SER oon tes-tah-MEN-toh /reh-see-BEER ehs-tray-mah-oon-see-OHN.*
Please send my body home on the next flight.	Por favor, manden mi cadáver a casa en el próximo vuelo.	*Pohr fah-VOAR, MAN-den mee kah-DAH-ver ah CAH-sah en el PROHK-see-moh VWAY-loh.*

EAT AND RUN

One of the pleasures of Latino life is snacking at a street vendor's stand. Ironically, it may be safer to eat at a roadside stand because you can supervise the chef. If the meat you order is boiling in oil, many of the bacteria and parasites will be dead by the time they hit your plate. If you avoid garnishes, you may survive the meal.

Good day, sir. What is that?	Buen día señor. ¿Qué es eso?	*Bwain DEE-ah seen-yohr. Kay ehs EH-soh?*
I can see it is meat.	Veo que es carne.	*VAY-oh kay ehs CAR-nay.*
But what species?	¿Pero de qué tipo?	*PAIR -oh day kay TEE -poh?*
I can't find that in my dictionary.	No encuentro eso en mi diccionario.	*No en-KWEN-troh EH-soh en mee deek-see-oh-NAH-ree-oh.*
Give me one anyway.	Déme uno de todos modos.	*DAY-may OO-noh day TOE-dohs MOE-dohs.*
No lettuce, for God's sake!	¡Por Dios! ¡Sin lechuga!	*Pohr DEE-ohs! Seen lay-CHOO-gah!*
Can't you see I'm a gringo?	¿Qué no ve que soy gringo?	*Kay no vay kay soy GREEN-go?*

PERFECTING THE HAGGLE

Merchants and vendors will think you're a fool if you pay their asking price. The markup for Yankees is roughly five times an asking price that is already doubled for locals.

Even with this 1000% markup, many things will still seem reasonably priced. Remember, though, that *you represent gringos and gringoland.* If you don't haggle, you'll make us all look thick.

These look well-made/delicious/ Martian.	Estos parecen estar bien hechos/ser deliciosos/ser Marcianos.	*EHS-tohs pah-RAY-sen ehs-TAHR bee-EN AY-chos/sair day-lee-see-OH-sohs/sair Mar-see-AH-nohs.*
How much for one/two/half a kilo?	¿Cuánto por uno/dos/medio kilo?	*KWAN-toh por OO-noh/dohs/MAY-dee-oh KEE-loh?*
Nine cents! Ridiculous!	¡Quinientos pesos! ¡Ridículo!	*Keen-ee-YEN-tohs PAY-sohs! Ree-DEE-koo-loh!*
If I had money like that, I would be vacationing in France.	Si tuviera ese dinero, estaría de vacaciones en Francia.	*See too-vee-AIR-ah EH-say dee-NAIR-oh, ess-tar-EE-ah day vah-kah-see-OH-nays en FRAHN-see-ah.*

Would you consider three cents?	¿Consideraría trescientos centavos?	*Kohn-see-dair-ahr-EE-ah tray-see-EN-tohs sen-TAH-vohs?*
No need for shouting.	No hay necesidad de gritar.	*No eye nay-say-see-DAHD day gree-TAR.*
I'll buy it next door. Good-bye.	La compro aquí al lado. Hasta luego.	*Lo COM-pro ah-KEE ahl LAH-doh. AH-sta loo-AY-goh.*
That's more like it.	Así está mejor.	*Ah-SEE ehs-TAH may-HOAR.*
Done. Thank you, madam.	Hecho. Muchas gracias, señora.	*AY-choh. MOO-chahs GRA-see-ahs, seen-YORE-ah.*
I'm thrilled to have saved four cents.	Estoy encantado de haber ahorrado doscientos centavos.	*Ehs-TOY en-kahn-TAH-doh day ah-BAIR ah-or-RAH-doh dohs-see-EN-tohs sen-TAH-vohs.*

POST WASTE

Hot offices and low pay ensure long lines and inefficient postal service. And on occasion, stamps are removed from letters—especially from goofy postcards—and sold again. Avoiding this hazard is simple: send letters *registrado*. The stamps will be canceled right in front of you.

I'd like to send this airmail to the United States.	Quisiera mandar esto via aérea a Estados Unidos.	*Kee-see-AIR-ah man-DAR EHS-toh VEE-ah ah-AIR-ee-ah ah ehs-TAH-dohs oo-NEED-ohs.*
Am I in time for the evening mule?	¿Llegué a tiempo para la mula de la tarde?	*Yeh-GAY ah tee-EM-poh PAR-ah la MOOL-ah day la TAR-day?*
Will it arrive by the turn of the century?	¿Llegará a fin de siglo?	*Yeh-gahr-AH ah feen day SEE-gloh?*
No guarantees?	¿Sin garantías?	*Seen gah-rahn-TEE-ahs?*
Actually, sending letters into the Void is one of my hobbies.	En realidad, mandar cartas al Vacío es uno de mis pasatiempos.	*En ray-ahl-ee DAHD, man-DAR CAR-tahs ahl vahs-EE-oh ehs OO-noh day meece pah-sah-tee-EM-pohs.*

ESSENTIAL EXPLETIVES

Although Wicked Travelers invariably know a few curses, they almost never need to use them. If you must curse a native, do so under your breath or on a very long-distance call—some Latinos feel obligated to kill people who question their honor.

What whoreness!	¡Qué putada!	*Kay poo-TAH-dah!*
Don't mess with me, tostada-face!	¡No me friegues, cara de tostada!	*No may free-AY-gayss, KAH-rah day toast-AH-dah!*
Watch it, you with the wife who gets around!	¡Cuidate, cabrón!	*KWEE-dah-tay, cah-BRONE!*
I'll grind you into little sausages.	Te voy a picar en pedacitos de salchicha.	*Tay voy ah pee-KAR en pay-dah-SEE-tohss day sahl-CHEE-chah.*
And feed them to your mother.	Y dárselos de comer a tu madre.	*Ee DAHR-say-lohs day coh-MAIR ah too MAH-dray.*

EL BANCO DE QUIXOTE

Thanks to the ubiquity of the ATM, you may never need to enter a Latin bank. If you do, though, the machine-gun-toting guards are not there to prevent robberies; their job is to keep frustrated customers from killing sluggish clerks and each other.

Getting angry won't speed up the service, and patience is often just as pointless. Vitriol at least makes us feel better.

Sir, let me warn you.	Señor, déjeme advertirle.	*Seen-YOHR, DAY-heh-meh ad-ver-TEER-leh.*
I've been waiting for half an hour.	Llevo esperando media hora.	*YE-voh ess-pair-AHN-doh MAY-dee-ah OR-ah.*
Cut in front of me and you're a dead man.	Cuélese y lo mato.	*KWAY-lay-say ee loh MAH-toh.*

Ladies. Excuse me for interrupting your fascinating chat.	Señoritas. Discúlpenme por interrumpir su plática tan interesante.	*SEE-nyoh-REE-tahs. Dees-KOOL-pen-may pohr een-tair-oom-PEER soo PLAH-tee-kah tan een-tair-ehs-AHN-tay.*
I'd like to exchange some dollars.	Quisiera cambiar unos dólares.	*Kee-see-AIR-ah kahm-bee-AHR OO-nohs doh-LAR-ehs.*
Oh, no! Don't send me to window seven!	¡Oh, no! ¡No me mande a la ventanilla siete!	*Oh, no! No may MAN-day ah lah ven-tah-NEE-yah see-ET-ay!*
I know perfectly well there is no window seven!	¡Sé muy bien que no existe la ventanilla siete!	*Say MOO-ee bee-EN kay no eks-EES-tay lah ven-tah-NEE-yah see-ET-ay!*
Don't point that machine gun at me!	¡No me apunte esa ametralladora!	*No may ah-POON-tay con eh-sah ah-meh-tra-ya-DOH-ra!*
Are you fools?	¿Están locos?	*Ehs-TAN LOH-kohs?*
Can't you see this is a good deal?	¿No ven que esto es un buen trato?	*No ven kay ESS- toh ehs oon bwain TRAH-toh?*
I'm offering you dollars for pesos!	¡Les estoy ofreciendo dólares por pesos!	*Lay ehs-TOY oh-fray-see-EN-doh doh-LAR-ehs pohr PEH-sohs!*

BANISHING THE MINIATURE HUCKSTER

Even hardened North Americans are shocked at the poverty in the Hispanic world, where not all beggars are adults, and some are actually cute. For a five-dollar donation, you will win a loyal following that will hound you like groupies around the clock. For those who cannot ignore importunate children, the following phrases are provided.

How old are you?	¿Qué edad tienes?	*Kay ay-DAHD tee-EN-ehs?*
Three is too young to be working.	Tres es muy chico para estar trabajando.	*Trehs ehs MOO-ee CHEE-koh PAR-ah es-TAR trah-bah-HAN-doh.*
Especially at midnight in a bar.	Sobre todo, en un bar a la medianoche.	*SO-bray TOH-doh, en oon bar ah la MAY-dee-ah-NOH-chay.*
Well, I don't need any Chiclets/ dolls/rugs.	Buena, no necesito Chicles/ muñecas/ alfombras.	*BWAY-noh, no nay-say-see-toh CHEE-klayss/ moon-YEK-ahs/ ahl-FOAM-brahs.*

Look. Things are tough all over, kid.	**Mira chavo. Las cosas están duras en todas partes.**	*MEER-ah CHAH-voh. Las CO-sahs ehs-TAN DOO-rahs en TOH-dahs PAHR-tayss.*
Okay, okay. Here's thirty cents.	**Okay, okay. Aquí tienes doscientos centavos.**	*Oh-kay, oh-kay. Ah-KEE tee-EN-ayss doh-see-YEN-tohs sen-TAH-vohs.*
Go buy yourself a condo.	**Ve y cómprate un condominio.**	*Vay ee KOM-prah-tay oon kohn-doh-MEE-nee-oh.*

REPORTING THEFTS

In many third-world countries, anyone with shoes and socks is a mark, and the only distinction between a cop and a crook may be a badge. Therefore, there are only two reasons to request a police report: to get a vacation souvenir and for insurance purposes. To get an officer's attention, you may have to reassure him.

I'd like to report a mugging/ burglary/ pickpocket/ car theft.	Quisiera denunciar un asalto/robo/ carterista/robo de auto.	*Kee-see-AIR-ah day-noon-see-AHR oon ah-sal-TOH/ROH-boh/cahr-ter-EES-tah/ROH-boh day ow-toh. Ess-PAIR-ay!*
Wait! Let me explain, please.	¡Espere! Déjeme explicar, por favor.	*Ess-PAIR-ay! DAY-hay-may eks-plee-KAHR, pohr fah-VOAR.*
I don't expect you to solve the crime.	No espero que resuelva el crimen.	*No ess-PAIR-oh kay race-WELL-vah el KREE-men.*
I do not expect to see my camera/ passport/money/ car again.	No espero ver mi cámara/ pasaporte/dinero/ auto de nuevo.	*No ess-PAIR-oh vair mee CAM-ar-ah/pah-sah-POHR-tay/dee-NAIR-oh/ow-toh day NWAY-voh.*

All I need is a piece of paper from you.	Lo único que necesito de usted es un papel.	*Loh OO-nee-coh kay nay-say-SEE-toh day oos-TED ehs oon pah-PELL.*
It is for the insurance company.	Es para la compañía de seguros.	*Ehs PAR-ah lah kohm-pan-YEE-ah day say-GOOR-ohs.*
Here is a little something for your trouble.	Aquí tiene algo por su molestia.	*Ah-KEE tee-EN-ay AHL-go pohr soo moh-LESS-tee-ah.*
That's okay. Don't get up.	Está bien. No se levante.	*Ehs-TA bee-EN. No seh lay-VAHN-tay.*
Thank you for your kind attention, sir.	Gracias par su amable atención, señor.	*GRAH-see-ahs pohr soo ahm-AH-blay ah-ten-see-OHN, seen-yohr.*

THE ETERNAL SIESTA

Spend one day in a hot, dry country and you'll begin to understand why nothing gets done between noon and three o'clock. You may even wonder how anything ever gets done.

But you may also begin to understand the many wonderful meanings of the siesta tradition.

The clerk is taking a vertical siesta.	El empleado está tomando una siesta parado.	*El em-play-AH-doh ehs-TAH toh-MAHN-doh OO-nah see-ES-tah pah-RAH-doh*
Our maid is on a permanent siesta.	Nuestra sirvienta está en siesta permanente.	*NWAY-strah seer-vee-EN-tah ehs-TAH en see-ES-tah pair-ma-NEN-tay.*
Excuse me, Beautiful. Would you join me for a siesta?	Disculpa, Guapa. ¿Quisieras acompañarme a una siesta?	*Dees-KOOL-pah, GWAH-pah. Kee-see-AIR-ahs ah-comb-pahn-YAR-may ah OO-nah see-EST-ah?*

MAÑANA COUNTERATTACK

The Latin character has a languid aspect that appears especially pronounced among restaurant staff. Your dagger-like stares and loud complaints may have no impact. But by changing the rules of the game, you can get a taste of the hot blood in the Latin heart.

Yes, we're leaving.	Sí, nos vamos.	*See, nohss BAH-mohss.*
We had a wonderful time.	La pasamos muy bien.	*La pah-SAH-mos MOO-ee bee-EN.*
We like you very much.	Nos cae muy bien.	*Nohs CAH-eh moo-ee bee-EN.*
Pay the bill?	¿Pagar la cuenta?	*Pah-GAHR la KWEN-tah?*
Hey, what's the hurry?	Oiga, ¿cuál es la prisa?	*OY-gah, KWAL ehs la PREE-sah?*
Aren't we friends?	¿Que no somos amigos?	*Kay no SO-mohss ah-MEE-gohs?*
Did you hurry for us?	¿Acaso se apuró para nosotros?	*Ah-CAH-soh say ah-poo-ROH pohr no-SO-trohss?*
We'll pay tomorrow!	¡Le pagaremos mañana!	*Lay pah-gah-RAY-mohss man-YAH-nah!*

EL BUSINESS MEETING

Business practices are different in the Spanish-speaking world. Conversations may be held at close range; even if you can see the pores on your associate's nose, you must not back away. This would be a serious loss of face. Likewise, you must hold eye contact like a gunfighter.

Latin businessmen are more comfortable with physical contact. If your counterpart squeezes your shoulders or fondles your lapels, do not be alarmed. He is probably just lonely.

Good afternoon, Mr. Honorable Senior Vice President Estrada.	Buenas tardes, honorable señor vicepresidente ejecutivo Estrada.	*BWAY-nahs TAR-dayss, ohn-or-AH-bleh seen-YOHR veece-pray-see-DEN-tay eh-hay-koo-TEE-voh Ehs-TRAH-dah.*
I have brought you some gifts.	Le he traído unos regalos.	*Lay ay try-EE-doh OO-nohs ray-GAH-los.*
This is a pen. This is a pencil.	Esto es una pluma. Esto es un lápiz.	*EHS-toh ehs OO-nah PLOO-mah. EHS-toh ehs OON LAH-peece.*
Do you like our company logo?	¿Le gusta el logotipo de nuestra compañía?	*Lay GOO-stah el loh-go-TEEP-oh day NWACE-trah kohm-pahn-YEE-ah?*

You didn't have to get me a gift!	¡No tenía usted que regalarme nada!	*No ten-EE-ah oos-TED kay ray-gah-LAR-may NAH-dah!*
Well, if you insist.	Bueno, si insiste.	*BWAY-noh, see een-SEES-tay.*
This is a fine ashtray. Such sturdy plastic!	Es un cenicero fino. ¡Un plástico tan resistente!	*Ehs oon seh-nee-SEH-ro FEEN-oh. Oon PLAH-steek-oh tahn ray-zees-TEN-tay!*
Go ahead! Try your new pen!	¡Ande!¡Pruebe su pluma nueva!	*AHN-day! Proo-AY-bay soo PLOO-mah NWAY-vah!*
Sign on this line, Your Excellency!	¡Firme aquí, Su Excelencia!	*FEER-may ah-KEE, soo ex-cell-EN-see-ah!*

LA REVOLUTION

Thanks to poverty and isolation, some people have missed the news about Stalin. If you are captured by revolutionaries, accept the fact that they are serious. Even if they speak in reverent tones about Mao Tse-tung, do not laugh. Just play along and hope somebody pays your ransom.

Brothers and sisters of the revolution!	¡Hermanos y hermanas de la revolución!	*Air-MAHN-ohs ee air-MAHN-ahs day la rev-oh-loo-see-OHN!*
I believe in your cause, whatever it is.	Creo en su causa, sea cual sea.	*KRAY-oh en soo COW-sah, SAY-ah KWAL SAY-ah.*
Down with imperialism/ colonialism/ capitalism!	¡Abajo con el imperialismo/ colonialismo/ capitalismo!	*Ah-BAH-ho con el eem-per-ee-ahl-EEZ-moh/coh-lohn-ee-ahl-EEZ-moh/cah-pee-tahl-EEZ-moh!*
Take my MasterCard!	¡Tome mi tarjeta de crédito!	*TOH-may mee tar-HAY-tah day CRAY-dee-toh!*
Buy yourselves some boots/ uniforms/ sunglasses!	¡Cómprense unas botas/uniformes/ anteojos oscuros!	*COMB-pren-say OO-nahs BOAT-ahs/oo-nee-FOR-mayss/an-teh OH-hos os-KOO-ros!*

HANDY GUIDE TO LATIN REVOLUTIONARIES

I n some Latin countries, armed conflict is a generations-old tradition. The names of the "revolutionaries" change, but their stated aim is invariably justice. Since that concept can include the torture and murder of civilians, it's worth knowing something about the local freedom fighters.

COUNTRY/ NAME	GOAL	LIKES	DISLIKES
Colombia/ FARC	Freedom for Drug Dealers	*Julio Iglesias* *Small bills* *Rocket launchers*	Extradition David Bowie Brooks Brothers
Peru/ Shining Path	Maoist Government	*Coca leaves* *Coca paste* *Staying up late*	Capitalism Democracy Holding jobs
Puerto Rico/ FALN	Puerto Rican Nationhood	*U.S. food stamps* *U.S. dollars* *Plastic explosives*	Actual danger "Gilligan's Island"
Spain/ETA	Basque Independence	*Jai-Alai* *Spicy fish sauces* *Killing policemen*	Spanish French Paying taxes

LOVE IN THE TIME OF SEVERE ABDOMINAL CRAMPS

A sophisticated traveler is able to woo a native on his or her own turf and in his or her own tongue. But special phrases are needed to deal with the unique challenges of a Latin love affair.

Ai.	Ai.	*Ai.*
You make me hot, my little chili pepper.	Me calientas mucho, chilito mío	*May cah-lee-EN-tahs MOO-choh, chee-LEE-toh MEE-oh.*
Am I in heaven or in hell?	¿Estoy en el cielo o en el infierno?	*Es-TOY en el see-AY-loh oh en el een-fee-AIR-noh?*
It you love me, my little refried bean, fetch the thermometer.	Si me amas, mi frijolito refrito, traime el termómetro.	*See may AH-mas, mee free-ho-LEE-toh ray-FREE-toh, tra-EE-meh el ter-MOH-may-troh.*
Yes. As I suspected.	Sí. Como lo sospechaba.	*See. COH-moh loh soas-pay-CHAH-bah.*
One hundred four and a half degrees.	Ciento cuatro y medio grados.	*See-EHN-toh KWA-troh ee MEH-dee-oh GRAH-dohs.*
I am near death.	Estoy cerca de la muerte.	*Ess-TOY SAIR-kah day la MWER-tay.*

Love me but once more before I die, my little empanada.	Amame una última vez antes de que me muera, mi pequeña empanada.	*AH-mah-may OO-nah OOL-tee-mah vase ahn-tes day kay may MWAIR-ah, mee pay-KAIN-yah em-pah-NAH-dah.*
Wait! Holy Mother of God!	¡Espera! ¡Santa Madre de Dios!	*Ess-PAIR-ah! SAHN-tah MAH-dray day dee-OHS!*
I must get back to the bathroom!	¡Tengo que volver al baño!	*TEN-go kay vohl-VAIR ahl BAHN-yoh!*

COCKFIGHTS

Among many rural
people, cockfight-
ing is honorable and
just. They know how mean
these birds really are and figure
the bastards have it coming.

The contests are not inher-
ently interesting, so everybody bets on which bird
will survive.

The cock was not brave/ fierce/lucky.	El gallo no fue valiente/bravo/ afortunado.	*El GAHL-yoh no foo-eh vah-lee-EN-tay/BRAH-voh /ah-for-too-NAH-do.*
He lost 10,000 pesos for me.	Me hizo perder diez mil pesos.	*May EE-soh pair-DAIR dee- ACE meel PAY-sohs.*
He had the fortitude of cheese.	Tuvo la fortaleza del queso.	*TOO-voh la for-tah-LAY-sah del Kay-soh.*
And the heart of a parakeet.	Y el corazón de un perico.	*Ee el kohr-ah-SOHN day oon pair-EE-coh.*
Now his stud days are finished.	Ahora sus días de semental han acabado.	*Ah-OR-ah sooce DEE-ahs day sem-en-TAHL ahn ah-kah-BAH-doh.*

BULLFIGHTS

Among aficionados, bullfighting is more art than sport, more poetry than cruelty. You can take comfort in the knowledge that the bull sometimes wins. If you want to be accepted in machismo company, toss around a few of the following phrases.

English	Spanish	Pronunciation
The picador is a villain!	¡El picador es un villano!	*El pee-kah-DOOR ehs oon vee-YAH-noh!*
The bull, he is handsome.	El toro es guapo.	*El TOH-roh ehs GWA-poh.*
He moves like a thundercloud across the landscape.	Se mueve como un nubarrón por el campo.	*Say MWAY-vay COH-moh oon noo-bahr-ROHN pore el CAHM-poh.*
His thing is like a tree trunk.	Su asunto es como un tronco de árbol.	*Soo ah-SOON-toh ehs COH-moh oon TRON-koh day AR-bohl.*
His brain is like a pinto bean.	Su cerebro es como un frijol bayo.	*Soo sair-RAY-broh ehs COH-moh oon free-HOLE BY-yoh.*

MARIACHI AT A DISTANCE

The joys of mariachi are elusive and mysterious. Yet we are endlessly subjected to the music by the well-meaning players who circumnavigate dining rooms like huge pests in sombreros. A few phrases can help us keep the players at a distance.

Hey! High-ya!	¡RRRijajai!	*RRRee-HI-HI!*
What loud costumes you have!	¡Qué trajes tan llamativos!	*Kay-TRAH-hayss tahn yah-mah-TEE-vohs!*
What forceful/ energetic/familiar music!	¡Qué música tan fuerte/enérgica/ familiar!	*Kay MOO-see-kah tahn FWER-tay/ eh-NEHR-hee-kah/ fah-meel-ee-AR!*
It's a lot of fun.	Es tan divertida.	*Ehs tahn dee-vair-TEE-dah.*
Now please get out of my face.	Ahora por favor de mi cara.	*Ah-OR-ah pohr-fah-VOAR day mee CAH-rah.*
Or I will bite your maracas.	O morderseré sus maracas.	*Oh mor-dare-SAR-ay soos ma-ROCK-ahs.*

THE POLITE GUEST'S GUIDE TO ENTRÉE IDENTIFICATION

People south of the border eat many animals not found in barnyards. When you receive your food, examine the sauce and then discreetly clear some away from a corner of the item in question. Note its color and texture and cut into it, noting toughness, internal features, and squirting or oozing. Then take a small bite and consider how it compares to more familiar food.

MEAT	SPANISH NAME	CHARACTERISTICS	COMMENTS
agouti	tepescuintle	*gamey, pork-like*	large rodent
armadillo	armadillo	*gamey, agouti-like*	may be road kill
Chihuahua	itzcuintli	*tiny claws*	special delicacy
goat	cabrito	*unusually greasy*	tasty if young
lizard	iguana	*chicken-like*	another edible pet
turtle	tortuga	*juicy, steak-like*	endangered species
worm	gusano	*worm-like*	deep-fried, crunchy

NATIVES AT HOME

E ven if you can jump the language barrier, you
may be confused by a Latino dinner invitation.
Nine o'clock doesn't mean 9:15 or 9:30 as it does
in English. It means 11. Once the conversation begins,
choose non-controversial subjects. Your host may
feel compelled to defend the honor of his ancestors,
his country, his wife, and her cooking skills.

Good to see you at last, General and Mrs. Hernández.	Qué bueno verlos finalmente General y Señora Hernández.	*Kay BWAY-noh VAIR-loh fee-nahl-MEN-tay hen-air-AHL ee seen-YOAR-ah hair-NAN-dez.*
Your apartment/ house is magnificent.	Su apartamento/ casa es magnífico(a).	*Soo ah-par-ta-MEN-toh/CAH-sah ehs mag-NEEF-ee-coh(cah).*
The heavy wooden/leather furniture is fine and austere.	Los muebles de madera/cuero son finos y austeros.	*Lohs MWAY-blayss day mah-DAIR-ah/KWAIR-oh sohn FEEN-ohs ee aust-AIR-ohs.*
The gold wallpaper is equally attractive.	El empapelado dorado es igualmente atractivo.	*El em-pah-pay-LAH-doh doh-RAH-doh ehs ee-gwal-MEN-tay ah-trahk-TEE-voh.*

THE MODEL GUEST

That was the best meal I've ever had after midnight.	Esa as la mejor cena que he comido después de medianoche.	*EHS-ah ehs la may-HORE SEH-nah kay ay co-MEE-doh dess-PWEHS day MAY-dee-ah NOH-chay.*
I'm so stuffed I don't think I have room for flan.	Estoy tan lleno que no creo tener espacio para el flan.	*EHS-toy tahn YAY-noh no CRAY-oh ten-AIR ess-PASS-ee-oh PAR-ah el flahn.*
No need for threats, General!	¡No hay necesidad de amenazas, General!	*No ay nay-SAY-see-DAHD day ah-meh-NAH-sahss, hen-air-AHL!*
Of course I'll have some!	¡Claro qua probaré un pedazo!	*KLAR-oh kay pro-bar-AY oon pay-DAH-soh!*

THE INEVITABLE THANK-YOU NOTE

The thank-you note is fast becoming a lost art, but civilized people still expect one. If a native has shown you hospitality, writing a short note (not a postcard) can smooth ruffled feathers and lead to fresh invitations.

Dear General Hernández,	Estimado General Hernández,
Thank you for the wonderful evening.	Gracias por una agradable velada.
That liquor was certainly strong!	¡Aquel licor era realmente fuerte!
I am sorry I mentioned politics/your wife's proportions.	Siento haber hablado de la política/de las proporciones de su esposa.
I admire military rule/ 300-pound women.	Admiro el gobierno militar/ mujeres de 140 kilos.
As a matter of fact, my own beloved wife is a dictator/ orangutan.	En realidad, mi propia esposa querida es una dictadora/orangután.
Thank you for canceling the death squad/duel at dawn.	Gracias por cancelar el escuadrón de fusilamiento/ duelo al amanecer.
Best regards,	Saludos,